SAMUEL LOGAN BRENGLE

Portrait
of a
Prophet

Samuel Logan Brengle

Portrait of a Prophet

By

CLARENCE W. HALL

Published by

THE NATIONAL HEADQUARTERS
THE SALVATION ARMY INC.
New York ∾ ∾ *N.Y.*

First printing 2,500 copies
Second printing 2,500 copies
Third printing 2,500 copies
Fourth printing 2,500 copies
Fifth printing (Memorial Edition) 10,000 copies
Sixth printing, 5,000 copies

MANUFACTURED COMPLETE IN THE U. S. A. BY
THE COLONIAL PRESS INC., CLINTON, MASS.

FOREWORD TO MEMORIAL EDITION

By General Evangeline Booth

In these days of stress and strain, when faith fails and hearts turn cold and purses are empty, and many who have put their trust in riches have learned that riches are deceitful, I am grateful to the God of all Grace that there should be this record of a long and faithful life, dedicated in absolute surrender to the service of God and man, and sustained until the fulness of years by the power of the Holy Spirit dwelling within the soul.

Even in the secular sense, these vital pages contain much of vivid human interest. There are glimpses of many scenes in many lands, nor will anyone who reads be in danger of losing interest for a single page.

But it is as a testimony to the Redeeming Blood of Christ that he whose portrait is here painted in such glowing colors would wish to be seen. If this book is destined—as I pray and confidently anticipate—to be a call of the people back to the Cross, it is because the Christ of the Cross summoned a soldier of Salvation to His bleeding side and sent him forth, under the Blood-and-Fire Flag, to fight the good fight against sin and suffering throughout the world.

Commissioner Brengle was a man of high principle, disciplined character, keen discernment and literary culture, who, in any walk of life, would have won personal respect and achieved an honorable success. But no biography of him would have been needed or heeded. What illuminates this narrative is the love that claimed these fine qualities for a task of noble and tender ministry. It was at Calvary that Samuel Logan Brengle discovered the upward path of a prophet which became his career.

It was a divine commission that he fulfilled as a Commissioner.

Many specifics are recommended in these days for the evil that undermines innocence and shatters self-respect. We hear much of psychology and other mental sciences. In the pathology of guilt, Commissioner Brengle stood out a distinguished specialist. He did not attempt to be himself the Great Physician. He brought to bear on the patient a healing influence greater than all the resources of man. He surrounded the victims of Satan with the presence of the Savior. He prayed until they prayed. He plead until they repented. Countless multitudes of men and women were drawn to him in their distress and appealed to him in their pain.

As an evangelist, in quietness and confidence was his strength. The peace of God which passeth all understanding was partner of the power of God that breaks down all resistance. Deliberately he avoided fine language and abstruse ideas. His words were simple as arrows flying to the mark. They pierced the hardened exterior. They reached the misery within. They were the surgery of the penitent-form.

Let a new generation study this book—appreciate its profound significance, acknowledge that the responsibilities here disclosed are not ended with the active career of the great champion of conversion. The old finish their course. Theirs be the glory in the Church triumphant. Let the young, marching forward in the Church militant, follow the example of this hero of Christianity, and put on the whole armor of God.

Evangeline Booth

GENERAL

September 1936

CONTENTS

CONTENTS

SAMUEL LOGAN BRENGLE

PRELUDE

"Your young men shall see visions . . ."

Moving along a scarcely discernible wilderness trail in southern Indiana, a "prairie schooner" is picking its way westward. Branches of the forest trees lean low, as though stooping to look more closely at this invading vehicle of civilization. Patches of thick-grown underbrush reach out from the sides of the trail, as though to feel with leafy fingers the wagon's mud-flaked wheels and tear with jagged fingernails its billowing canvas.

A man and woman occupy the only seat, just back of the straining flanks of the horses. The man is full-bearded and square of jaw; beneath the brim of his shapeless hat are eyes that connote restlessness, eyes that have a way of focusing themselves upon far horizons. Though the woman's visage is of softer texture, her appearance is that of a woman whom frontier hardship can mark but not deface, fag but not coarsen.

Immediately behind them, alternately standing to ejaculate over some unfamiliar object along the way and sitting back again upon pieces of household bric-à-brac, are two boys, bare of foot and freckled of face. One of them, addressed as "Sam" by the other, is about eight years of age.

They are "movers,"—though historians will later refer to them by the more genteel word "pioneers,"—one of many families following the receding line of the frontier, seeking richer farm land, blacker soil, with its promise of a greater yield of corn to the acre.

Packed in the wagon, tied on and around it, are all their worldly possessions. Inside are beds, a few chairs, a bureau, a rough table or two roped together. Outside, swinging and jangling with every jolt and lurch of the wagon, are pots, pans, kettles, axes, plowing implements. The wagon creaks under its load, and, when the going is hard, Sam follows his half-brother and stepfather over the side to walk ahead, leading the horses.

Soon the lengthening shadows from the great oaks and beeches indicate that it is time to camp for the night. The horses are turned into a clearing and unhitched. A few things necessary for supper and sleeping are unpacked. The woman busies herself with the pots and pans, and the boys gather wood.

After supper, Sam's mother opens the Bible, and all are silent while she reads a portion by the light of the campfire. The reading is from the Book of Genesis; it has to do with Abram's going into another land, an unknown place. The lesson is aptly chosen; it is good to dwell upon such passages; it helps to make the "movers'" going easier. One verse especially strikes into the boy Sam's imagination; it is:

Look now toward heaven, and tell the stars, if thou be able to number them: and He said unto him, So shall thy seed be.

For the benefit of the boys, the reading is explained in simple, primer language: the man Abram, listening to the calling of God, is to become, he is told, the father of children, "spiritual" children, so numerous that they would be like the stars for number!

But the boy Sam does not understand. Like the stars? How could that be?

And that night, lying on a straw pallet thrown from the wagon and placed for the boys beneath the trees, he stays awake for hours, looking up through the leaves to the twinkling stars high above. The words of the Bible reading turn and twist in his mind. The man Abram . . . doing God's will . . . becomes the father of many people . . . like the stars. . . .

What does it mean?

CHAPTER I

GENESIS

ON JUNE 1, 1860, a record clerk in the little village of Fredericksburg, Indiana, picked up his pen, noted the date, and scribbled a concise entry in his register. What he wrote was:

"Born, this date, to William Nelson and Rebecca Anne Brengle, a boy: Samuel Logan Brengle."

Had the clerk been a man of prophetic imagination, or at least a student of genealogies, he might have garnished his bare and brief record with certain facts. He could have shown, for example, that the frontier's latest-born had emerged from an ancestral background not undecorative to New World history; that the tiny heart of the infant Samuel was pumping blood which was red with the traditions of pioneers, of men and women who had figured honorably, if not prominently, in the early American scene.

The Brengles came to America in early Colonial days. Tingling in their souls were love of God, love of liberty, love of adventure. They settled at first in Maryland, but hearing later of a land to the south and west, a land of beautiful hills and rich valleys, tall forests of timber lands and plenteous game, ample plains and roving buffalo herds, warm climate and clear-running waters alive with fish, they set out in quest of a new home.

The Maryland Brengles reached the wilds of Ken-

15

tucky in 1763, thirteen years before the Declaration of Independence, and six years before Boone brought his family to Kentucky to live. Settling on eighteen hundred acres of choice land, they made their clearing, built their log cabins, filled their lungs with air no white man had breathed before, and fell to the task of making the fertile soil provide them with a living. Between times they fought Indians, wolves, bears, mosquitoes and malaria.

Among the pioneers of Kentucky who had "arrived" there grew up a saying—a deep-chested, bushy-browed, boastful saying: "The cowards never started, and the weak ones died on the way." The Brengles had arrived. They could meet and become intimate with hardship, privation, suffering. They could blaze trails, extend borders, push back frontiers. They could go into depths and over heights hitherto unexplored, and leave a trail plainly beaten, plainly marked, for the weaker ones to follow. Then the weak ones would not have to die on the way. Then even the cowards would be encouraged to make a start.

George D. Brengle, son of the Kentucky-conquering contingent of 1763, and grandfather of Samuel Logan Brengle, lived in Fredericksburg, Kentucky, where he did well both as a blacksmith and as a progenitor. At his smithy was a growing, thriving business; in his home were eleven children, also growing, also thriving. Equipping all his children with the best education available in the backwoods schools of the day, George Brengle urged them to follow the dictates of their individual likes and dislikes in choosing careers. Two became preachers: James achieving a measure of renown as pastor for more than thirty years of the Presbyterian Church in Corydon, Iowa, where his name and memory are still revered; while Logan, independently minded, gave hurt to his mother's staunch Presbyterian heart by turning aside from the church of his fathers to take a preaching commission from the new-born, Methodist-conceived United Brethren Church, explaining his rash action by saying simply, "I felt led that way."

William Nelson, seventh child of George Brengle, turned to teaching as a profession. Because his mouth smiled less and his eyes sought books more than did those of his brothers and sister, he was singled out in childhood as the gravely sedate one of the family. Growing to manhood, he moved from Fredericksburg, Kentucky, to Fredericksburg, Indiana, where he took charge of a school.

In the village young William Nelson Brengle soon became regarded as an outstanding citizen. Men idling around the village store nodded their heads, spat, caressed their beards with bony hands on which the veins stood out like whipcords, and pronounced the schoolteacher a brainy, level-headed fellow, with a deep earnestness about him. Women remarked that, while Mr. Brengle was not exactly handsome, there was something about him that made folks turn for a second look when they passed him. Not the least of the indications of the esteem in which the villagers held him was that he, though a Presbyterian, was elected superintendent of the Methodist Sunday school, which he attended in lieu of a church of his own denomination.

Among the families whose children came to the little log schoolhouse to be taught by the young pedagogue were the Horners. They had moved to Indiana from the Carolinas, and were upright, God-fearing, thrifty folk; fervent, warm-hearted Methodists. The Horners had nine children. Of these, two went to California, seeking with thousands of others the gold that men declared might be washed with sieves out of any creek. Two others turned to the practice of medicine; the youngest, named Samuel, saying he wanted to become a doctor because he "just couldn't bear to see folks suffer." Rebecca Anne, one of the girls, went to school under William Nelson Brengle.

William Brengle had not been teaching long in the presence of the pretty Horner girl until he found he was developing for her, in spite of himself, a disturbing affection not of an academic character. Love blossomed, and soon the monotony of life in Fredericksburg was broken by the announcement of the betrothal of "Horner's girl" to the school-master.

The marriage was the outstanding event of months. The whole village attended. After the ceremony came the customary "infare," and then William Nelson Brengle and his bride, with the well-wishes of the villagers ringing in their ears, began life together in the little white cottage next to the school.

The days and months passed. Summer faded into fall, fall gave way to winter, winter thawed into spring. And with the coming of nature to life again, the spring of the year 1860 spoke new things to Rebecca Anne Brengle.

The first day of June brought the fulfilment of her dreams. And when the weariness of her great giving was over, she named her first-born Samuel Logan: Samuel, after her youngest brother, who became a doctor just because he "just couldn't bear to see folks suffer"; and Logan, after her husband's brother, who dared to seek a preaching connection outside the family faith simply because he "felt led that way."

Chapter II

BOYHOOD

EARLY in his life the grim figures of war and death came close to the boy Sam Brengle, leaving indelible impressions upon his memory.

When he was only about two years old his father left for the war. William Brengle, with an older man, had recruited a company of volunteers from the village, and when the older man was made Captain, Brengle was made First Lieutenant. During the following months Lieutenant Brengle saw considerable service, was captured once, but escaped. Soldiers, wounded and sent home to recover, talked about his bravery, about what a disciplinarian he was, and told of how capably, when the Captain was absent on furlough, he had led his men in the fight.

Little Sam listened with no little pride to these stories of his father's courage and ability, taking delight in picturing him in all his dignity of authority and uniform at the head of brave men. But when, after long months, his father came home it was as an invalid; during the siege of Vicksburg he had been laid low. He lived but a short while; then one day Sam was taken into his mother's arms, while she explained between sobs: "Papa has gone to be with God."

Death, moving on footsteps silent as the fall of night,

had come close and explained itself to Sam as a sort of ally, a grim ally, of God.

After William Brengle's death, Sam and his mother lived alone in the cottage next to the schoolhouse for two and a half years: mother and son; two natures very close. When his father went away to war, she had taken over the school, and had proved as popular as a teacher as she had been as a neighbor; the children loved her and responded readily to her gentle discipline.

After school Rebecca Anne Brengle would take her boy with her on long walks; together they would explore the woods, rest among the trees, stroll along the banks of the Blue River, pick blackberries and hazel nuts. She loved nature, loved to listen to the singing of birds, to the movements in the brush of all God's wild creatures. Sam came to realize that these things spoke to her of God, of peace, of a Land Beyond; that they had voices that sounded in her ears like echoes of comfort and promise from the Bible, to which she had constant recourse and whose stories she would read to him in the evenings.

Life was not hard financially. William Brengle had been thrifty, had saved enough to buy two small houses in the village; in one of these they now lived, while the other brought in a little each month as rent. Then, too, there was the pension which widow and son received as dependents of an officer who had died while in his country's service. This, augmented by an amount from her father's estate and the small income from teaching, provided Rebecca Anne Brengle and her boy with enough to live on comfortably.

Then one day Sam's mother called him aside to tell him a secret: she was to be married again. The man who was to take his father's place was a good man, a doctor; and he had two children, a boy and a girl, company for

Sammy. Life would be better, more interesting for them both, she told him.

But in the days and months following the wedding Sam saw and heard things which told him that his mother had not bettered their affairs by her marriage. Anxiety, caused by unusually hard work and by the struggle to keep enough to eat on the table, wrote new lines into her face. He saw, too, that she had less time to devote to him now. And he began to feel lonely. Requests for story-telling brought only the tired response, "I haven't time now, Sammy; I'll give you a book of stories some day when you can read." Around the village Sam occasionally heard his family classed with "poor folks."

Sam noticed, too, that his stepfather had a way of picturing success and better times as always just ahead. Doctoring was not profitable; he would do better at farming. But with farm land a-plenty around Fredericksburg, he explained that it would be better to try elsewhere. He proposed a move "over a ways in Indiana"; there corn land would be richer, blacker, capable of yielding more bushels to the acre. Always, as Sam was to find out through several such changes, better times were "just over a ways," on the horizon, tomorrow.

In the early autumn of 1868 the move was made.* A farm site had been chosen near Harrisonville, between 75 and 100 miles from Fredericksburg. After a short sojourn here, another move took the family to a farm near Shoals, Indiana.

Out on this farm, where he and his family and poverty all dwelt together, Sam Brengle rapidly became intimate alike with learning that comes from textbooks and knowledge that comes from living close to mother earth.

---

* Referred to in the Prelude.

School was held only three or four months of the year, and that during winter. To farmers seeking to wrest a living from lands cleared of heavy forests, schooling for their children had to be a secondary consideration; from spring to harvest children had to help on the farm; winter, its severe weather making farm work impossible, was the only time to think of education.

Through snow up to his knees Sam trudged to and from the rude school-house. Here, while he struggled with the three R's, he trembled from cold and fear of the rod. The school-house was like the homes: a log cabin with puncheon floor and a great open fireplace into which it was the boys' job to roll huge logs for the fire. Those who sat near the fire were almost roasted; those farthest away shivered.

Games and sports evoked in Sam a keen delight. He discovered that he was becoming strong. He liked to feel the play of his muscles, hardened by work in the fields, and to test their strength in wrestling, tugging, scuffling, in games embodying rough and tumble combat. His prowess soon became recognized, and he was pointed out as a good fellow to have on one's side.

Between the short sessions of school he learned to bend his back to guiding the plow, to pulling fodder, to harrowing a field of grain, to wielding an axe. He came to know the feel of aching muscles, of hands that became rough and blistered before becoming callous, of sleep that descended like a benediction after long hours of arduous labor.

The first money he ever earned was for harrowing a neighbor's land—forty cents a day for four days brought to him possession of $1.60, a fabulous amount that made him feel "richer than Vanderbilt."

Familiar to his ears were all the sounds of the farm

and the conglomerate chant of the prairies; the metallic tinkle of cow bells, the grunting of hogs, the cackle of chickens, the croaking of frogs on the river-bank, the chatter of blue-jays and the sharp staccato of red-headed wood-peckers and the "who-who" of the big night owls.

His nostrils knew the autumn odor of moist soil on a frosty morning; the springtime odor of loam with the push of new life in it; the vital summer odor that comes with the breeze sweeping through the tall, succulent prairie grass; the scent of free-growing prairie flowers.

Life on the farm, withal, was drab and lonely. It was the drabness of sameness, the same things done over and over, the same few people to see and hear and talk to, the same "corn-pone" and fried bacon to eat, the same round of planting, plowing, pulling weeds, with the same exhausted feeling at the end of the day.

And so he came to know silence—the silence of wilderness loneliness, farm loneliness, little village loneliness. And silence taught him to depend for company upon his imagination and his books. With these he could companion; he took them with him into the field, communed with them behind the plow. He would let them talk to him down by the river while lying in the shade of a great oak or hickory, a wisp of straw in his mouth, bare toes, clay-colored, moving meditatively. And amid the sounds of running water and whispering leaves his thoughts and dreams would build themselves into airy realities. Like the water, his thoughts could run on and out—out to far places, out to only God knew where. Like the leaves, his spirit could feel the move and sway of unseen forces that were none the less powerful for their intangibility.

Because the prairie pictures before his eyes were flat and colorless, he developed the ability to make pictures behind his eyes. Across inner vistas he would parade characters from the books he had read over and over again while "sitting on his shoulder blades" with his feet on the trunk of a tree, or lying flat on his stomach before the open fireplace. And in many a day dream, unalloyed by mundane things such as plows and prairies, furrows and frontiers, he would make his favorites perform again and again their action of the pages.

His books were not many; pioneers had small libraries. Besides the Bible—whose stories, awesome prophecies, comforting assurances, and rhythmic phrases were as familiar to him as was the village gossip concerning persons, politics, crops and religion—there were a few other books that helped to create the pictures behind his eyes. These included "Pilgrim's Progress," Plutarch's "Lives," Stephen's "History of Methodism," Dickens' "Pickwick Papers," the works of Josephus, Scott's "Ivanhoe," and a "History of our Wars."

His constant reading and re-reading developed gradually within him a love for the vehicles of expression. Lyrical phrases, euphonious words, musical sentences—these pleased his inner ear as his mind-pictures pleased his inner eye. So avid was his desire to know that, when he had read and read again all the other books on the shelf, he would take down Webster's Unabridged Dictionary and find fun in toying with words and their meanings. He would try them out on stumps and cornstalks and furrows, and then take them to bed with him to brood over their meanings.

An inner eye that could make pictures in his head, and an inner ear that could hear and enjoy and pursue words and their meanings—these were Sam Brengle's possessions as a boy, possessions which then helped to relieve the monotony of prairie life, later made of him an orator, a painter of word pictures, and later still helped to make of him a preacher of power, with the ability to present vividly and realistically the tragic terrors of hell and the transcendent delights of heaven.

By the time Sam was twelve, years and growth had laid their hands upon him, toughening his sinews, hardening his fibres, lengthening his bones, running through his body the changing forces of adolescence. More important is it, however, that by now another element had wrought its work upon him, tracing its lines, invisibly but permanently, in the thoughts of his brain and the affections of his heart.

That element was religion.

His earliest and keenest, though perhaps fragmentary, recollections of this period are connected with attendance at meetings. In company with his mother and stepfather, he went regularly to the little church a mile or more from his home. He had noticed that "goin' to meetin'" was a prominent feature of the life of prairie dwellers, that church and what it stood for was almost their only release from a dreary existence.

Sam knew from experience that vital godliness, sane and satisfying, had a cornerstone prominence in the lives of his own and many other families. He had seen men and women, notorious as sinners, kneel at the mourners' bench and get up saying they were saved. Afterwards he had noticed that going to "preachin'," reading the Bible, saying grace before meals, having family prayers in the morning and at bedtime, had become part of their daily round. He had seen men and women, referred to by their neighbors as "good Christians," return good for evil, turn wrath away with soft answers, love their enemies.

Sam could watch these manifestations, and could say

to himself that they tallied with his mother's teachings. Wrought into the pattern of his soul by the weaving fingers of her training was a reverential fear of God. It was this fear of God that was responsible for his having so far kept himself clean. He was no born prodigy of saintliness. Within him were the same sly drawings and tempting inclinations toward evil that are to be found in any normal boy. More, he felt the movings of a capacity for wrong-doing, a consciousness of inward fires, smoldering deep down, capable he knew of springing into consuming flame, that kept him constantly afraid. He heard of men and women falling into gross sin, of men flying into fits of rage and killing others, and at times the movements within him made him feel of kith and kin with all transgressors, leading him often to wonder whether he would not do as much or more if put in their places and faced with their temptations.

Occasionally he had flare-ups of violent temper. One day, with resentments flaming, he flung hot words of anger at his stepfather, who he felt had been unfair in a certain demand. Sam's mother, standing by, said nothing, only looked at him. But that look caused him bitter sorrow, of which he would write a half century later:

Her look of grief I can still see across the years. It was the one sad memory of my childhood. A stranger might have been amused or incensed at my words, but mother was grieved—grieved to her heart by my lack of generous, self-forgetful, thoughtful love.

The idea that conversion—that mysterious something he had seen revolutionize the lives of neighbors after going to the mourners' bench—would change his desires and strengthen him in temptation, first came to him while attending a Methodist church meeting one evening in the fall of 1872. It was a few months after his stepfather, acting upon another moving impulse, had packed up the family and their belongings and moved across the Indiana state line into Illinois, settling on a farm about eight miles from the village of Olney. On this particular evening Sam was an attentive listener to the sermon. Always oratory—whether pulpit, political, or of any other kind—had fascinated him. But in the midst of the sermon, when suddenly the preacher's face became lighted with an unutterable glory, Sam forgot elocution and was seized by the thought that he would like to be a Christian. No call being given, however, he made no start.

Several months later, at a revival meeting in the little Methodist Episcopal church, Sam, with some school chums, was sitting on a rear bench. The invitation to "come and get religion" had not been repeated many times before Sam abruptly arose and betook himself to the altar, where he sank to his knees among others, some moaning, some weeping, some shouting. The prayers his mother had taught him did not seem to fit here, so he listened for some suggestions from those praying aloud. Adopting some of their words and phrases, he uttered a prayer, and then waited, fully expecting a new and strange impetus to lift him to his feet where he would leap and shout, as others had done. Nothing, however, happened to him; no thrill, no feeling.

Not intending to be denied the experience he had set his heart upon, Sam for five successive nights made his way to the mourners' bench. He was not there among the penitents because of any profound conviction of sin; he simply felt that he should be a Christian, that it was his duty to take a definite stand before his fellows; that by so doing he somehow would gain strength. That the

Lord did not visit him with some spectacular acceptance, he considered strange. Since he was "only a boy," nobody came to help him; and besides, the rule was to let the Spirit do all the work. The room being heavy with heat and without ventilation, Sam dropped off to sleep on one or two occasions while waiting for something to happen.

On the fifth night, which was Christmas Eve, Sam's mother knelt beside him. She said but little, only telling him that now that he had come forward publicly and given himself to God, he should "trust." Still no feeling. When he was asked to testify, he scarcely knew what to say, and had to depend again upon the vocabulary of those he had heard talk under similar circumstances.

Weeks passed, with nothing to tell him he was a Christian except that he had gone to the mourners' bench. Then one night, while on his way to prayer meeting, there came the "witness." He and his mother, walking together across the broad and desolate prairie, were talking about a proposed move to Texas that had been given up some months ago. Sam, musing on this recent decision, said, "I'm glad we didn't move to Texas, Mother. If we had, I might have fallen in with a rough, drunken lot of fellows, and lost my soul. But we have stayed up here, and I have become a Christian." Scarcely had the words left his lips when there came into his heart an inexplicable feeling. Not an inrush of glory, not a sweeping sensation of having entered some seventh heaven; but a sweet, deep, pervasive sense of peace, quietness, rest, blessedness. Instinctively he knew now that God had accepted him. Though he had heard no voice, it was as though something had just been said to him, loud and clear, something that had settled once and for all any doubt as to whether he had a right to call himself a Christian.

For days, weeks, months, Sam walked in the enjoyment of an exquisite sense of God's favor, anxious to show to the whole world, and more especially to his boy companions, how Christ-like his life was henceforth to be. In the flush of his new life, he felt that it was virtually impossible for him to want to be other than like his Master.

Then one day he discovered in himself the presence of something that did not want to act like Jesus. That disturbing revelation came to him one afternoon when he, with three other boys, was going home from school. While playing along the way, one of the boys took offence at something done by Sam, and, drawing angrily away, called him an opprobrious name. It was a name which, among boys, always called for one of two things: retraction or a fight. In a flash Sam forgot he was a Christian, or ignored the fact, and struck the offender a swift blow. Because the other did not strike back, there was no further trouble between them. There was, however, trouble elsewhere: in the soul of Sam the light had gone out. Instantly, with the striking of that blow, the inward witness had been withdrawn. Conviction of sin now flooded his heart; and with the vanishing of the sense of God's favor, a sense of Divine displeasure overwhelmed him.

In time, after much sorrowing and praying, he got back his consciousness of peace and forgiveness. But he had become possessed of a new and disquieting knowledge: there still remained in him a something that under provocation would make him act unlike his Lord. There was no one then to tell him that the carnal nature can be destroyed, that constant victory is a possible experience.

Hence, eight years must pass before he would be rid of the continual struggle to keep his experience, and to act at all times like Jesus.

Meanwhile, he found work his most potent weapon against temptation. If only he could keep busy!

There began for him a life of religious activity. He had already joined the church and entered enthusiastically upon its life. In addition, he took up systematic reading of the Bible, also devoting himself with greater care to the study of his Sunday school lessons. So thoroughly, indeed, did he prepare the latter that his grasp of them attracted attention, and one day when the teacher of the men's Bible class was absent from duty, fifteen-year-old Sam Brengle was asked to take his place.

Some months later, when the church had need of an assistant superintendent for the Sunday school, and the name of Samuel Logan Brengle was proposed, he was unanimously elected.

Assistant superintendent of the Sunday school! Pondering the new responsibility that was his, he told himself that it involved careful conduct, much study of the Bible, more determined efforts to master the unChristlike proclivities within him. The feeling that he was now a pillar of the church, with an important segment of the sanctuary resting upon his shoulders, provoked the thought that for the sake of others he must not stagger; he must be strong.

And this thought became a bulwark against the moving, laughing, sneering remnant of his old nature that would, if given a chance, rise up to overthrow his experience.

Helpful, too, was the necessity for concentrating upon his studies. The hunger to know, the power and leadership which he saw come to those who did know—these made him determined to acquire all that was possible to him of the learning of the schools. Having gathered all that the little country school could offer him, he enrolled in 1874 as a student of the Olney high school.

Especially was he interested in grammar—the right use of words, their meanings, their marshalling into phrases and sentences that set the mind singing and dancing as do the melodies of an orchestra. He wanted to know how to handle words, how correctly to use them so that, when put on paper or printed in books, they would create pictures a boy could carry behind his eyes, or, spoken from the lips of an orator, could echo and re-echo in a boy's head in rhythm which would transform even plowing and harrowing into agreeable tasks.

Sam attended the Olney high school for one year, at the termination of which he was told by scholars and teachers, who had perceived his avidity for grammar, that he should go to a Professor Hinman at Claremont, seven miles from Olney. Hinman, they said, was a crank on the subject, a specialist in words and phrases. A few months later, Hinman took Sam into his own home, where he treated him as a younger brother and where these two devotees of speech and its parts consorted for two years and began a close friendship that lasted to the day of Hinman's death.

But now, fifteen miles from home, the distance making impossible the regular week-end visits to his mother that had helped to break his spells of loneliness when in Olney, Sam became subject to more and more frequent attacks of the "blues." Coils of melancholy wrapped their moody abstractions about him; often he felt he must die of homesickness. Unable to withstand any longer the desire to see his mother, he hired a horse one Saturday and rode home. Mother's tight embrace and her tears told him the longing had been mutual. He stayed over night, and at sunset the next day kissed her goodbye, listened to her final "Be a good boy, won't you, Sammy?" and rode away, half turning in the saddle to wave farewell until a turn in the road shut her from his view.

It was, indeed, farewell. The following Wednesday he received his first telegram; it read, "Come quick. Mother dying." Bewildered, he started for home, but when home was still a mile away, a neighbor halted him to say he was too late; his mother was dead. That remaining mile's journey would ever live with him as the longest he ever traveled.

Sam remained for the funeral, listened to the thud of the heavy clods upon the wooden casket, and walked away from the grave with a lost look showing dully through his tears. Lonely before, he was bereft now. During the next few days, before returning to school, he rambled distractedly through wooded places, seeking solace in the embracing shadows.

The months and years ahead would find him without a place he could call home; lonely, silent often, brooding, bereft. On many a winter's evening, when he looked out at the black sky and blanketing snow, he would say to himself that he knew something of the feelings of the earth at being in the grip of a cold and icy hand.

Chapter III

THE CALL

Following his mother's death, Sam, under the wise and patient tutelage of Professor Hinman, devoted himself with new intensity to his studies. Idleness, he found, brought spells of melancholy; therefore, he sought to keep himself busy at the task of improving himself. He found, too, that the more he fed his hunger for knowledge, the more his appetite for it increased. And with his increasing desire to know, there grew up in him a fervent ambition to succeed grandly in some important work, to write his name high on some peak of world endeavor.

However vague might be his plan for his life work, there was nothing vague about his understanding that achievement along any line is made easier by a liberal education.

He therefore set about procuring the necessary funds to go to college. Some money had been left to him by his father, which his stepfather, following his mother's death, was caring for as his guardian. But Sam's request for some of this money for college expenses was summarily disapproved, his stepfather saying that college was a waste of time. Nevertheless, Sam was insistent, and was about to take steps to force the issue when he received word that his guardian had moved away, taking his money with him, but leaving him the farm. The sale of the farm was handled for Sam by a lawyer friend, and thus the way was opened.

Accordingly, in the fall of 1877 when the new term began, he crossed over into his native state and enrolled at Indiana Asbury University*, a Methodist Episcopal school located at Greencastle, Indiana. Not having acquired the requisite amount of high school credits in Olney, it was necessary for him to put in two years in the preparatory school connected with the university before matriculating for his college work.

One of his first acts upon arriving in Greencastle was to join by letter the College Avenue Church, where he regularly attended worship throughout his college career. Equally claimant on his interest was the Sunday school class with which, at the invitation of the leader, a senior in the university, he affiliated himself early in his first year at Asbury, later in the year being elected teacher by the class members. For five years he led this class, built it into one of the largest and livest of the church, and in time led every member, without exception, to a profession of faith in Christ as Savior and Lord and to membership in the church.

It must not be thought, however, that because they are here given first mention, church-going and Sunday school teaching filled his college days, or even that they had first claim upon his affections. These he performed conscientiously as duties, not as delights. Brengle's chief interest, as might be suspected in one with his ambition, lay in another direction. His prime reason for coming to the university was not to save souls, but to expand Brengle. The medium he had chosen for that expansion was oratory.

Why this subject, above all others, should interest him is not strange when it is remembered that at this particular period oratory was having its greatest day. It was

---

* Changed in 1882 to DePauw University.

the era of big words and lyric phrases. Speeches fared out by politicians and preachers the country over smacked of glitter and dazzle. Being heard throughout the land were the mellifluous voices of such master "spell-binders" as Prentiss, Beecher, Phillips, Conkling, Blaine, Hill, Ingersoll. America was astir with eloquence on fire and pyrotechnics set to words; audiences demanded speech with flame in it.

In young Brengle, oratory found a faithful zealot. With an assiduity born of intense love, he would respond diligently to her demands for long hours of study and practice. A speech with a prize at stake often would require months of memorizing, cultivation of voice, rehearsal of gestures. For years he made it his practice to sit at a piano or organ, often for hours at a stretch, striking the tones of the scale and following them with his voice, thereby developing gradually a resonant, organ-like tone, with depth, flexibility, and volume.

When preparing a speech he was careful in his choice of words; they must be tuned to the particular effect he wanted his speech to register. Especially did he like sonorous words of the type that would give his voice tones full play.

Brengle had not gone far with his studies in the arts of speech before rewards, one by one, began to fall into his lap. By the time he had advanced to the freshman degree in the university proper he could look back with pride upon a long list of achievements on the platform. Through his public speaking he attracted attention to himself, became popular and widely-known among the undergraduates. He was voted into the university's chapter of the Delta Kappa Epsilon fraternity, which counted among its members then, no less than now, many distinguished and yet-to-be distinguished men of affairs.

After winning so consistently in inter-class oratorical contests that there was scarcely a chance for any other student to take a prize, Brengle represented his university with honor and success in various state competitions, being pitted against some of the ablest men of the Middle West. Oratory being what it then was, this activity brought him into the limelight much as is the case with college gridiron stars in the present day.

Into what vocation oratory might eventually lead him, he had not seriously thought. He had settled that public speaking was the vehicle of his destiny. The vehicle was the thing; the road down which it was to travel and the terminus it would reach were but incidental. As he approached twenty-one, however, he began to look at possible vocational roads. How about law? He had observed that most of the great prizes of life—political prizes, prizes of statecraft—came to lawyers. He had noted that in the places where were carved the names of the mighty there seldom appeared that of a business man, no matter how successful he might be. The majority of the molders of public opinion and makers of nations whose names were given high place in national esteem had come up through politics, no few beginning as lawyers.

Above every other vocation law seemed to make the loudest bid, appeared to offer most of those things his heart now craved: fame, position, wealth. Debating the subject with himself, he admitted that he wanted men to speak his name about the entire country as his fellow students did at the university. He wanted to achieve fame—fame that would last—fame that would carry his name throughout the land, to the whole world, down to posterity.

Law, then, it should be.

Among Brengle's intimates in the Delta Kappa Epsilon

fraternity at DePauw University were men who in the course of years were destined to write their names large in world affairs.

One of these chums was a Japanese student named Sutemi Chinda.* Quiet, mysterious, holding behind his almond-shaped eyes more wisdom than he spoke, the man from the Orient captured from the first the interest and friendship of the man from the prairie. Brengle engineered Chinda's acceptance into the fraternity, taught him to play chess, introduced him to the ins and outs of college politics.

Another friend and fraternity brother was a nervous, ambitious youth who had signed himself Albert Jeremiah Beveridge,† but whom his fellow "Dekes"—as the Delta Kappa Epsilons are known—hailed as "Bev." Popular and friendly with all, there was none with whom he was more fraternal than Brengle. They had a great deal in common, these two. Both had become widely-known; both were almost inordinately ambitious; both were looking forward to political careers.

When Beveridge first came to the university, eyes sparkling with aspirations, and saying, "I would be willing to go to hell if I could make a reputation as great as that of Napoleon," Brengle "spiked" him for the fraternity, recognizing in Beveridge a nature affined to his own.

On many an afternoon these two could be seen in the fraternity hall, Brengle, the senior in age and class, drill-

---

* Count Chinda: Japanese diplomat; Ambassador to Germany (1908); Ambassador to U. S. (1911-1916); Ambassador to Gr. Britain (1916-1920); Privy councilor and grand steward to Prince Regent; Japanese representative at Versailles Peace Conference (1919).

† Orator; U. S. Senator; Biographer of John Marshall, Abraham Lincoln, etc.

ing Beveridge in oratory, telling him his voice had wonderful possibilities once a certain harshness and lack of refinement of tone was overcome, correcting his gestures, making him put force and unction behind his words.

Candor of thought and feeling on all subjects was a hallmark of their companionship. One day, in discussing religion, Brengle told how he had gone to the mourners' bench five times, and had experienced nothing; and how one night, when coming across the lonely prairie, a Witness at length had spoken to him, giving him evidence which, though perhaps it would not be allowed in courts, had satisfied all questionings in his soul, and forever silenced the "prosecuting attorney" within. That was language that embryonic lawyers could understand, and the result of this talk was that one night, at a revival meeting being held near the university, Brengle led Beveridge to the altar, and later to church membership.

Between classes these two strolled the campus together, taking of oratory, politics, their law ambitions. Perhaps, they confided, when both were graduated they would together practice law, together seek the prizes of statecraft, remain pals with one goal. Now and then, however, Brengle would shake the foundations of these air castles by telling Beveridge of the peculiar leanings and drawings toward the ministry which he felt at times. Somehow, he would say, he could not get away from the haunting thought of his father having been called to preach, but having drawn back; of his parents having dedicated him to the ministry when he was only a babe; of the fact that whenever now he heard a preacher expounding the Word, it rang in his ears with almost irresistible appeal.

The days passed. Brengle was in his last term at the university. To this point in his life, the idea of preaching —"the Call"—had followed him, flitting across every horizon he created, intruding itself in the midst of his most roseate dreams, sounding like a distant echo in every valley of his vision.

Then in the fall of 1882 the Call stepped out of its obscurity, blocked his path, demanded a decision.

It happened in Providence, Rhode Island, where Delta Kappa Epsilon was having its annual convention. An important matter—one involving the very life of the De-Pauw chapter—had to be brought before the convention, and Brengle, as the chosen delegate from his university, had come half way across the country to attend. In order to solicit the support of other chapters, he had spent considerable time on the way, stopping off to visit many of the leading colleges between Greencastle and Providence.

He was met at his destination by the delegates from a chapter particularly opposed to his, who informed him flatly, "We will fight you to the death." Going to his room in the Narragansett Hotel, Brengle felt the weight of his mission. Never before, he told himself, had he undertaken a task so responsible. His own destiny, the destiny of his fraternity chapter, the very honor of his university, depended, he felt, upon his being able to carry the convention.

Heavily burdened and scarcely able to collect his thoughts for the attempt he had to make to save his chapter, he went out into the street, walked awhile, and then came back to his room where, exasperated by this inexplicable depression, he threw himself upon his knees and besought God to help him win. He seemed, however, to gain nothing by the exercise; his soul was lonely, and within all was dark as night. He rose, went out on the street again, returned, knelt again, prayed again. Still the loneliness, the depression, the darkness. Yet a third time he went out on the street, returned, prayed. While praying this time, the thought of preaching was suddenly presented to his mind. Considering the idea irrelevant, he sought impatiently to shake it off—but without success. A tremendous inner battle occupied the following minutes, but when at length he exclaimed aloud, "O Lord, if Thou wilt help me to win this case, I will preach!", the whole room seemed instantly to flame with light.

The next day, his soul bathed in a peculiarly comforting feeling, he went to the convention hall, delivered his speech from the floor, offered his motion, and to his intense surprise the very men who had sworn they would fight him "to the death" rose to support the motion that meant reinstatement and recognition for his chapter. His victory was sweeping and entire. Furthermore, after the session many crowded about him to say that if the convention had not already been organized that speech would have ensured his being elected its president.

Back at the university, he told Beveridge of his experience, winding up with: "So you see, Bev old boy, I've got to preach!" Beveridge, notwithstanding the evident force of his friend's conviction, did not prove tractable. For an hour he argued, reminded Brengle of their dreams and ambitions, created new visions of fascinating brilliance, and said again and again, "Sam, you'll be a fool to go into the ministry!"

But the die was cast. God had kept His part of the contract made in the Providence hotel. Brengle, too, would keep his.

With his life's work now clear before him, almost feverishly Brengle devoted his time to preparation for the ministry. The careful studying and teaching of his Sunday school lessons during the past four years had helped him. With others of the students, he established a noonday prayer meeting; some of the professors came in to take part; and a tangible and satisfying result was that a revival—later to be appraised as one of the greatest ever to shake the university—was born and flourished for months.

He began now to take preaching engagements, spending no little time preparing his sermons. These he wrote out in full and committed to memory, as he did his orations. Preaching once in the university church, and several times in various other places, he soon attracted attention. The presiding elder of the Greencastle District of the Northwest Indiana Conference, who knew Brengle's record as a student orator, heard him on one occasion and forthwith told him that he would obtain for him an appointment in the Greencastle District after graduation.

Graduation day arrived, and Brengle was duly presented with the sheepskin stating he was a Bachelor of Arts. Packing his trunk, putting his written-out sermons in his Bible, and shaking hands with the faculty and the students, he bade farewell to the university.

Beveridge accompanied him to the train, paced the station platform with him while they talked over their respective ambitions, and as the train was pulling out, shouted, "I'd give a fortune if I could be as sure of being in the United States Senate as I am that you will be a bishop!"

Chapter IV

CIRCUIT-RIDER

A SOLITARY figure on a horse, head bent low to shield his face from the icy blizzard blowing wild across the raw prairie. . . . Snow falling fast from a dull gray sky, obliterating the road ahead and blinding the horse, whose legs sink knee-deep into the drifts. . . . The man hugging his coat tighter, his mouth open to speak an encouraging word to his mount, one hand clutching the reins, the other holding a Bible against his breast inside the coat.

Such could be the essential lines of a sketch drawn to depict the Reverend Samuel L. Brengle, A. B., in 1884, when fulfilling engagements as a circuit preacher of the Methodist Episcopal Church, Northwest Indiana Conference.

It was to this circuit—comprising two villages, Brookston and Chalmers, and two country appointments—that Brengle was assigned following an unsuccessful attempt by the presiding elder of the Greencastle District to place him in a desirable little city church with a brand-new parsonage, which, true to his promise, he had reserved for him. But the bishop had overruled the presiding elder's plan. The idea of placing in this excellent charge "a youngster, who has not borne the burden and heat of the day, who is not married and therefore does not need a parsonage," was not compatible with the bishop's sense of the fitness of things.

While the thought of the city church with its new parsonage and cultured congregation had appealed strongly to him, Brengle was not many months on his circuit before he realized that both happiness and spiritual stature had come to him through that appointment. Years later he said in retrospect:

Losing that city church was the best thing that could have happened to me. If I had gone to that appointment to work among those cultured and refined people, I should have swelled with pride, tried to show off my spread-eagle oratory, and doubtless would have accomplished little. But out among the comparatively illiterate and uncultivated farmers of my circuit, I learned the foundations of true preaching: humility and simplicity.

So thoroughly did he give himself to his circuit that before the year of his appointment was up he had achieved so much that others joined Beveridge in the prophecy that one day this man would be a bishop.

At the termination of his year on the circuit, Brengle, on the advice of Bishop Joyce—formerly his pastor in Greencastle and now a prominent church leader—decided to add to his ministerial qualifications by taking up studies at a theological seminary. Desiring to see something of the East, and also to have the experience of living in a large city, he chose Boston Theological Seminary, then one of the three great Methodist seminaries in America.

His education at the university had exhausted all the money he had received from his father's property, and he had been able to save but little from the pittance paid him by the poor people of his circuit; therefore he was forced to borrow money for the venture. Two friends came to his aid with $500: William Switzer, now a preacher himself; and a Greencastle banker, a member of the church in which Brengle taught a Sunday school class for five years. Asked what security he wanted, the banker replied: "I will take your face as security, Sam. Just give me your note. I will trust you, and you can pay me when you can."

Thus, led on by his ambition to become a great preacher and to write his name high in ecclesiastical circles, Brengle set out for Boston Theological Seminary, where he so diligently worked toward his goal that fellow students, passing his room, would pause to say: "Still at it, Brengle? When do you sleep? Your light is burning when we go to bed, and it is burning when we get up!"

Meanwhile, across the ocean in England a strange religious movement had sprung up and was spreading rapidly throughout the British Isles. Heading the movement, having accepted the title of General, and describing his Army as "moral scavengers, netting the very sewers," was a tall, angular man who people said had a voice of thunder and a heart of flame. The saving of sinners was his passion; redeemed men were to be his soldiers; of the sinners he said: "We want all we can get; but we want the lowest of the low."

The methods the General had adopted to "carry on the war" had become the scandal of churchmen and the delight of the common people and toughs. The latter, gathering here and there into bands under the name of "The Skeleton Army," had raised disturbances of all kinds. Salvationists were being mobbed, thrown into prison, brick-batted, rotten-egged, mocked, derided. On the head of the General were being poured such epithets as "tub-thumper," "brazen-faced charlatan," "pious rogue," "masquerading hypocrite," "cunning scoundrel." "Well meaning, but mad—stark mad" was the verdict of the more tolerant.

Despite all, however, the movement was thriving. On letter paper, printed in 1877, appeared the heading "The

Salvation Army," with the subhead "called The Christian Mission." There, too, were listed the 47 "principal stations"; in each of these a favorite song being sung had these ambitious words:

Hark, hark, my soul, what warlike songs are swelling
  Through Britain's streets and on from door to door;
How grand the truths those burning strains are telling
  Of that great war till sin shall be no more!
Salvation Army, Army of God!
Onward to conquer the world with Fire and Blood.

William Booth, having belted Britain with his zealous bands, now was turning his nervous eyes farther afield. Soon his Army would be on its way to America. Brengle, now on a train headed for Boston, would meet it there. No glimpse of the vista immediately ahead being afforded him, he thought that Boston was for him just another step toward his new ambition: the title of Bishop. Indeed, many years afterward, when thinking of this high aspiration and what happened to it, he would laugh and say: "If I had thought when I was on my way to Boston that I was ever going to join a tatterdemalion Army of that kind, I probably would have dropped off the train at some river and drowned myself!"

CHAPTER V

PENTECOST

BREAKING through the windows of Boston Theological
Seminary on the morning of January 9, 1885, the first
streaks of dawn faintly illumine the figure of Brengle,
seated in his room, head in hands, elbows on his study
table. He is up and dressed early this morning for a
particular reason. For several days conviction that he
should be sanctified has lashed his soul into restlessness,
rendering sleep almost impossible; for weeks he has
searched the Scripture, ransacked his heart, cried to God
almost day and night. Today, he tells himself, he must
obtain—or be lost forever.

No longer does he doubt the existence of such a blessing.
Through exhaustive study under the personal guidance
of Dr. Daniel Steele,* he has become mentally persuaded
that sanctification is a doctrine gloriously possible of in-
carnation in human life.

Others who have by their precept and practice helped
to smother his former doubts concerning the possibility of
holiness are Wesley, Fletcher, and more recently, Dwight
L. Moody, Dr. William McDonald, and Catherine Booth.
Of the last-named, whose books, "Popular Christianity"
and "Godliness," he has recently read and digested, he can

* Then Professor of Didactic Theology, Boston University, and
one of the world's foremost authorities on the Greek New Testament.
Noted author of books on the Higher Christian life.

46

say: "She seems to unsheathe a Damascene blade. Her sword is the sharpest I have ever known any preacher to wield."

In his search after holiness, he has been aided, too, by his membership in the Octagon Club, a religious coterie not unlike the "Holy Club" founded by Charles Wesley at Oxford in 1729, which was the embryo of the Methodist Church. The Octagon Club is composed of a select group of the more intellectual students, who meet each morning for prayer and the discussion of religion in its deeper manifestations. Among the members are some who avowedly have been seeking sanctification, Brengle one of them.

Under a variety of terms—Holiness, Sanctification, Perfect Love, Second Work of Grace, Baptism of the Holy Spirit, Blessing of a Clean Heart, etc.—he has seen this experience written about, expounded, testified to. He cares not, however, for terms. He envisions the experience as a precious gift from God. More, he sees it as a part of God, a person, Whom he does not now possess. He wants a whole God. Just as in the days when lawyer ambitions filled his mind he wanted all of law, so now that he is to be a preacher he wants all of grace. Gradually, however, he has come to see that only empty hands can grasp a whole God.

And the emptying of his hands has taken time.

Examining himself during the past several weeks, he has seen his heart to be studded with subtle bits of selfishness, proud little ingredients of the great big "I" in him. When he compared himself with his Lord he saw how woefully lacking he is in essential humility, self-effacement, self-abnegation. Let him tell it:

I saw the humility of Jesus, and my pride; the meekness of Jesus, and my temper; the lowliness of Jesus, and my ambition; the purity of Jesus, and my unclean heart; the faithfulness of Jesus, and the deceitfulness of my heart; the unselfishness of Jesus, and my selfishness; the trust and faith of Jesus, and my doubts and unbelief; the holiness of Jesus, and my unholiness. I got my eyes off everybody but Jesus and myself, and I came to loathe myself.

The more closely he has looked at himself the more diametrically opposed to the spirit of the Cross has he seen the "I" in him to be. Seeing the "I," therefore, and feeling its insidious, overmastering power, he has hated it and, bit by bit, has cast it from him.

Even in his seeking the Blessing, the "I" endeavored to cross his wires so that, hearing the voice of his own ambition, he might mistake it for the voice of God. For example, after listening to Moody, whose simplicity and power stirred him deeply, the thought had come: "If I can only be a great preacher like Moody! He ascribes his power to the Baptism of the Holy Spirit. Perhaps if I seek this Baptism, I shall have this power!" But even as he held the thought the Light of the Spirit had fallen upon it, revealing its grossness, and he threw it from him as an unholy thing, saying later: "I was seeking the Holy Spirit that I might use Him, rather than that He might use me."

Yet now, wrestling alone in his room at the break of day, he finds that the battle is still with the "I." The "great preacher" ambition dies hard. It clings tenaciously, pleading all manner of plausible apologies for life. With a chameleon-like aptitude it endeavors again and again, under the piercing Light, to change its color to match with holy ambition.

Let us look closely at this inner battle, note the subtle arguments of the "I," and see how the Spirit progressively breaks them down:

It would be as a great preacher, Brengle tells himself, that he could best reflect glory on God; and is not the glorifying of God the chief end of man? The Light flashes,

showing him that God can best be glorified through the
winning of souls.

Granted, Brengle agrees; the more souls saved the more
glory for God. Hence, to save many, he must have a large,
influential ministry. But again the Light flashes and,
seeing the "I" still smeared all over his aspirations, Brengle capitulates: "Lord, if Thou wilt only sanctify me, I will
take the meanest little appointment there is!"

So far, good. Yet he still has something left of the "I."
The thought comes that, even though his following shall
be small, he can still be eloquent, a powerful orator, building up his small section of the Kingdom of God through
the sheer force of his rhetoric and the cadences of his voice.
Yet again, however, the Light flashes; and now we see the
final gesture that empties his hands, as he casts away the
last segment of the "I." Listen: "Lord, I wanted to be an
eloquent preacher, but if by stammering and stuttering I
can bring greater glory to Thee than by eloquence, then
let me stammer and stutter!"

Let me stammer and stutter! Surely here is the final
step in self-surrender for this man whose every waking
moment and every sleeping dream since boyhood has been
toward the refinement of the arts of speech. So hungrily
does he yearn for complete cleansing and holiness that the
very vehicle of his destiny is thrown upon the altar. Later,
in telling of his triumph over the "I," he will say: "I was
willing to appear a big blunder and a complete failure if
only He would cleanse me and dwell in me!"

Stripped now in self-renunciation, he fully expects the
Spirit to clothe him with His presence. Nothing, however,
happens. Though his hands are empty, his heart is still
hungry. Emptied of self, he is, nevertheless, not yet filled
with God. Where is his blessing? What is the technique
of finding it? Worried at the ineffectiveness of his efforts,

elbows leaning hard on the study table, he gropes in spiritual darkness. And suddenly there comes up from his heart a voice speaking words that are old, but that bear a gloriously new meaning:

If we confess our sins, He is faithful and just to forgive us our sins, and to cleanse us from all unrighteousness.

". . . to cleanse us from all unrighteousness!" The words break across his heart like a sky rocket, illuminating the fact that since God is "faithful and just" his promised blessing must now be received by simple faith in those attributes of God's character. Instantly the Grace and faithfulness of God dawn upon him, and as he drops his head in his arms and murmurs confidently, "Lord, I believe that!" a great sense of peace flows over his soul.

Is this the Blessing? He need not put the question twice. Like a great, wordless, all-enveloping "YES!" he gets the answer from every chamber of his body and soul. It is as though all nature, visible and invisible, had nodded its head in testifying assent, and in the next instant has begun the movement of a cool, refreshing breeze within him and started springs of sparkling waters bubbling up all through his being. Whereas all previous blessings have been transitory, coming and going, this experience has the "feel" of permanency.

His throat emits no shout, his feet do no dance, but his face registers unmistakably what has happened. One of the students to whom, twenty minutes after his experience, he returns a book he borrowed yesterday, looks sharply at him: "Sam, what is the matter? You look so different!"

Another student, George A. Coe, later to become one of America's foremost modernists, teaching in turn at Northwestern University, Union Theological Seminary, and Columbia University, catches a glimpse of him coming down the stairs and afterwards tells him, "Sam, I saw you about twenty feet away, on the stairway, and the moment I saw you I said to myself 'Something has happened to Brengle!'"

Such, then, was the manner in which he, who was to become a chief exponent of the doctrine, entered into his own experience of heart cleansing.

On the street next morning he bumped into a man known about town as "the Hallelujah coachman":

> I told him of my experience. He jumped up and down for joy, and said, "Brother Brengle, preach it!" He and I walked out across Boston Commons. He talked and I listened. He couldn't speak a dozen words without butchering the Queen's English, but I was hungry enough now to listen to anybody. As he talked I took on courage, and said: "By the grace of God, I will preach it, if they throw me out of the church afterwards!"

The next day, Sunday, preaching in the Egleston Square Church, where he was student pastor, he took his text from Hebrews 6: "Therefore leaving the principles of the doctrine of Christ, let us go on unto perfection."

When he had preached his sermon, he told the story of his Pentecost. The crowd was visibly moved, and some came forward to say, "Brother Brengle, if that is holiness we want it."

The testimony apparently blessed many. But most of all it served as a Rubicon to him. It put him on record; it cut down all the bridges over which, had he not publicly declared himself, he might have slipped back. Angels in heaven, devils in hell, men on earth—all now had heard him say, in effect: "See? God has purified my heart. He has cleansed me from all unrighteousness. I am crucified with Christ. Henceforth I am dead to the world and the world to me!" He could not go back. He must go forward.

Thus once again a sense of responsibility for being an

example, for publicly declaring himself had saved him, made God smile, devils frown, and men watch.

Two mornings after his sanctification the honeypots were spilled into his heart. He had honored God; He had stood the test of fearing faithful witness. And since His man had exercised fullness of faith, God would now vouchsafe to him fullness of feeling. He has mirrored this experience for us in the following:

I awoke that morning hungering and thirsting just to live this life of fellowship with God, never again to sin in thought or word or deed against Him, with an unmeasurable desire to be a holy man, acceptable unto God. Getting out of bed about six o'clock with that desire, I opened my Bible and, while reading some of the words of Jesus, He gave me such a blessing as I never had dreamed a man could have this side of heaven. It was an unutterable revelation. It was a heaven of love that came into my heart. My soul melted like wax before fire. I sobbed and sobbed. I loathed myself that I had ever sinned against Him or doubted Him or lived for myself and not for His glory. Every ambition for self was now gone. The pure flame of love burned it like a blazing fire would burn a moth.

I walked out over Boston Commons before breakfast, weeping for joy and praising God. Oh, how I loved! In that hour I knew Jesus, and I loved Him till it seemed my heart would break with love. I was filled with love for all His creatures. I heard the little sparrows chattering; I loved them. I saw a little worm wriggling across my path; I stepped over it; I didn't want to hurt any living thing. I loved the dogs, I loved the horses, I loved the little urchins on the street, I loved the strangers who hurried past me, I loved the heathen—I loved the whole world!

Was it a mere vision, a momentary exultation, that a calmer moment would dissolve? Ten, twenty, thirty, forty, fifty years would pass, and yet he would give that same fadeless testimony, winding up with:

God did all that for me, bless His holy Name! Oh, how I had longed to be pure! Oh, how I had hungered and thirsted for God—

the living God! And He gave me the desire of my heart. He satisfied me—I weigh my words—He satisfied me! He has become my Teacher, my Guide, my Counsellor, my All in All!

Concerning his sanctification, of which the "glory experience" was only an incident, he has given us this record:

I have never doubted this experience since. I have sometimes wondered whether I might not have lost it, but I have never doubted the experience any more than I could doubt that I had seen my mother, or looked at the sun, or had my breakfast. It is a living experience.

In time, God withdrew something of the tremendous emotional feelings. He taught me I had to live by my faith and not by my emotions. I walked in a blaze of glory for weeks, but the glory gradually subsided, and He made me see that I must walk and run, instead of mounting up with wings. He showed me that I must learn to trust Him, to have confidence in His unfailing love and devotion, regardless of how I felt.

News of Brengle's sanctification spread. It was no light-under-the-bushel matter with him. He proclaimed it far and wide by his actions, appearance, words.

Two friends, high up in ecclesiastical and academic life, came to him. The first was a prominent Methodist bishop who had written a book on Christian Perfection, lived for a time as he wrote, then lost out. Hearing of Brengle's experience and preaching, the bishop sought him out one day to say, "Brother Brengle, be very careful. That doctrine splits churches."

The second man, Professor Phil Baker of DePauw University, came for a different purpose. Under the guise of paying a friendly visit, he spent several days with Brengle, watching him closely, questioning him. Then one day he burst into tears, saying: "Sam, the object of my visit was to find out if this experience of sanctification is

real. It is. And I have come to get it too." Down on their
knees together went the professor and his former student;
they prayed; and the professor went back home, a thousand miles, with the Blessing.

Manifest as were the signs Brengle's friends everywhere
saw of his transition from the carnal to the holy, however,
it was in his preaching that the change most radically appeared. Here we see a difference that should be carefully
noted, a change that was as revolutionary in nature as that
which occurs in the conversion of the vilest of sinners.
For no less grace was required to transform the ambitious
and self-seeking young preacher into the self-effacing
humble apostle of holiness, than is needed to save the most
besotted drunkard. Certainly no less; perhaps more. Let
us see:

Before sanctification, preaching meant honors for Brengle; now it was to mean glory for Christ. Hitherto preaching meant exaltation of self; now it would mean exaltation
of a Savior from self. Previously he preached to please;
now he would preach to disturb. Whereas his sermons
made men say, "How beautiful is his oratory!", hereafter
they would cause men to exclaim, "How black are my
sins!" The same voice, the same tones, perhaps the
same words, tickling the ears of the people, would now
drop into an audience with the cleaving power of a sword,
dividing his hearers into two opposite camps, compelling
a choice of sides. For he had forsaken preaching as a
profession, a medium for money-making and fame-accru-
ing, and adopted it again as a calling, a life passion, that
would have as its only object the saving of men and women from lowest sinfulness to highest sainthood.

To Brengle, Pentecost had come. Now he had a whole
God. And now God had a whole Brengle.

CHAPTER VI

PASTOR AND EVANGELIST

In the fall of 1885 came William Booth, paying his first visit to America. A minor hall in Tremont Temple, Boston, was filled with preachers, several hundred strong, who had gathered to see and hear at first hand just what this General of the much-publicized Salvation Army was like. Brengle, as student pastor of one of the city churches, was seated with the others awaiting the entry of the General.

The preachers were retailing stories they had heard of Booth and his Army. Brengle told, with a laugh, of the picture created in his mind when first he heard of the new organization and its leader. "I was only seventeen, a student in DePauw University, when I read a flippant little paragraph in a paper about a strange religious army that had risen in England under the leadership of one William Booth, a long, lank, bearded man who had been dubbed 'General.' I pictured to myself a man with flowing hair and beard, astride an old horse, and equipped with long military boots, fired with unreasoning, Saracenic fervor, and riding about England followed by a tatterdemalion crowd." Though this impression had vanished with the years, he told the preachers, he had subsequently developed a keen interest in the exploits of the irrepressible General. Moreover, he was not ashamed to confess that from somewhere down deep in his Methodist-trained soul

55

there had come an eager response to this religion with its dash and enthusiasm, depth and devotion—a response that the stiffening crust of higher learning and sophistication could not altogether stifle.

As they talked, a side door was swung open. A man in parsonic robes appeared first, followed by the tall, gaunt form of The Army's Founder. Over the latter's chest streamed an iron-gray beard; his military tunic was open, exposing a flaming red guernsey on which was worked a large, blazing crest with the words "Blood and Fire" fairly shouting at the observer. As with great strides the General reached the platform, Brengle's eyes swept over his figure. To him the slightly bent form, the gray hair and beard, and the seamed face appeared to corroborate all he had heard of The Army's fierce battles with the powers of sin—drunkenness, harlotry, degrading evils of all kinds, ridicule, haughty aloofness of churchmen, sullen opposition of municipalities. Though unable to take his eyes off the General, Brengle burst into tears at the sight of him, declaring to himself, "Here, certainly, is God's greatest servant upon earth today, the man bearing the heaviest burden of the world's sin and shame and woe."

Meanwhile, William Booth, with his virile address and his quiet, comprehensive answers to questions—many of which Brengle felt were not asked in either the spirit of brotherly love or of honest inquiry—carried his critical audience by storm. When the meeting was over, Brengle moved up with others to shake the General's hand. Coming abreast of that flaming crest with its "Blood and Fire," he murmured a wistful "I wish I could join you." This the General either did not hear or did not take seriously, since he gave no reply other than a pressure of the hand.

That night the General conducted an "all night of prayer," in which, among others, one of Brengle's fellow students, Charles R. Brown,* was converted. Brengle attended, and his allegiance to the General was still more securely cemented. The following day he was again touched by an address which Booth, at the invitation of Sam's chum, Hayes, gave to the students of the Theological Seminary.

After Booth had gone, days came when Brengle felt more and more the urgency of beginning at once upon his full-time ministry. The necessity for spending long hours probing the subtleties of theology, the casuistries of seminary classrooms, the adaptations and embroideries of dogma and creed, the application of science's light and scholarship's criticism to the whittled-down fine points of religion—these began to irk him.

In the midst of his urge to be up and doing there came a brilliant and tempting offer. Out in South Bend, Indiana, a man named Clement Studebaker, builder of wagons and of a fortune that had soared into many millions, had recently builded also a beautiful church, claimed by South Benders to be the finest Methodist edifice in Northern Indiana. In casting about for a suitable pastor, Studebaker had appealed to Dr. Gobin, vice-president of De-Pauw University, for a recommendation. Dr. Gobin had written by return mail: "Brengle is the man you want." A few days later Brengle was surprised by receiving three letters, one from Dr. Gobin, another from the district superintendent of the Methodist Church, and a third from Studebaker himself, each asking him to accept the pastorate of the "Studebaker Church."

What an offer! Here was honor, here a way out of the debt into which he had had to plunge to come to Boston and the seminary, here a large and wealthy congregation, here an immediate and instant leap over the poor appoint-

* Later dean of Divinity School, Yale University.

ments and small memberships and perplexities that have
to be hurdled by the average preacher before reaching so
desirable a goal. But he made no hasty decision. Better
hold his answer in abeyance for a few days, he reasoned
within himself, until he could return to earth, think clearly,
pray intelligently.

Meanwhile, taking a recess from his studies to ponder
the matter, he attended a holiness convention in Baltimore. Dr. G. D. Watson, whose books he had read with
blessing, was the preacher, and the convention was under
the general leadership of his friend, Dr. William McDonald. Ten days he spent thus, reveling in the rich and
searching expositions given by Watson.

On the Sunday morning, having been asked to preach in
the oldest Methodist church in Baltimore—the Utah
Street Church—he conducted a service whose fruitful results did much to swing him toward the course God had
laid out for him. It was at this period that Brengle felt a
definite call to evangelistic work.

That it was a call, and not simply a home-grown impulse of his own desire, was evident by the way he received it: he was staggered at the thought, offered argument against it, to which the vision of the beautiful and
affluent Studebaker Church added force. Feeling, however, that the call was coming directly from God, he just
as directly appealed his case to God: "Lord, I am $500 in
debt for my education, and the people in New England
where I am living now do not know me. If I go into
evangelistic work, how can I go about the country preaching holiness with these debts unpaid? The people may not
give me enough money to pay them."

On the one side: the Studebaker Church, with its big
salary, its important place, its wide pulpit. On the other:

evangelistic work, with its prospect of debts, uncertainty, itinerancy. How could he decide?

The Holy Spirit came to his aid. His mind was led to Jesus' words in the sixth chapter of Matthew: "Take no thought, saying, What shall we eat? or, What shall we drink? or, Wherewithal shall we be clothed? . . . your heavenly Father knoweth that ye have need of all these things. But seek ye first the Kingdom of God." The Spirit then took him over into Exodus, where he was reminded how God had led out from under the iron hand of Pharaoh a million Israelites with their wives, children, herds, and fed them for forty years in the wilderness. Thus pliant to the Spirit's guiding, Brengle thought he heard God Himself whisper to his heart: "Can you not trust Me? If I could care for those Israelites in a desert land, cannot I supply all your needs in rich New England?"

The question was settled. Out came pen and paper, and soon a letter was on its way to Mr. Studebaker in South Bend; in this letter the Reverend S. L. Brengle declined with thanks the flattering offer of the pastorate of "the finest church in Northern Indiana."

This decision marked his definite cut with pastorates and seminaries.

God was still at work, molding His man. And it is interesting to pause here for a survey of this most recent stage of his development. See how he has changed in his attitude toward evangelism! Back in his pre-Pentecost days of ministerial ambitions and self-seeking, he had confided to a friend that "the job of an evangelist seems to me to be beneath the dignity of a full-orbed man." But how now? He sees his calling in a new light; his job has become magnified. Catching a view of the Pauline assignments, he notes that there were "some apostles, some

prophets, some evangelists, some pastors and teachers,"
and writes from his new viewpoint:

> If we judge the importance of his [the evangelist's] work in the
> mind of God by the place Paul assigns him when he mentions the
> various orders of the ministry, then he stands next to the apostles
> and prophets, and before the pastor and teacher.

What a contrast there is, too, in his unction. Now that
Christ completely possesses him and the Holy Spirit altogether indwells him, a great passion for the saving and
sanctifying of all men burns hot within him. That passion has dissolved all thoughts of a career, of position, of
ministerial preferment. Forthwith he will address himself, with a devotion that knows no lessening, to the high
enterprise of an evangelist to the poor.

Returning to the seminary, Brengle packed his belongings and moved them out to a camp-meeting where he had
been invited to preach. Here the presiding elder of the
North Boston District of the Methodist Church heard him,
was impressed, and approached him with an invitation to
"conduct meetings in every church in my district during
the coming winter." Brengle accepted with elation, and,
going to his first appointment in the district, began with
high prospects his career as an evangelist.

During the next months doors opened on every hand.
Churches, camp-meetings, holiness missions, became eager
to secure his services. His engagements seemed to be made
for him by Divine appointment. Hundreds were converted
and sanctified under his preaching. At the insistence of
C. E. Cullis and Joshua Gill, the latter the associate editor
of the *Christian Witness,* he tried his hand at writing.
One of his articles was published in Cullis' *Times of Refreshing,* reappeared immediately in tract form, sold by
the thousands, and was republished in Canada, England

and India, causing Cullis to say: "It was the greatest seller we ever had." Dr. McDonald, president of the National Holiness Association, editor of the *Christian Witness,* preacher, author and publisher, also became devoted to Brengle, took him along as assistant in many of his great campaigns, helped him, pushed him forward. For ten months Brengle lived in a whirl of evangelistic activity and success.

There was, none the less, still another step he must take before he had reached the place for which God had been training him. Hints of his Lord's purpose for him came to Brengle at times—such as, for example, when he would pass a Salvation Army open-air meeting, or conduct a campaign in an Army hall, or associate in other ways with the uniform, bringing again and again that persistent whispering in his heart of the thought: "These are my people!"

The taking of that step was just ahead.

Chapter VII

MARRIAGE

Concerning the question of his marriage, the Reverend Samuel Brengle had prayed a prayer, set up a standard, and received an answer.

The prayer, oft-repeated, was first made shortly after his sanctification. On his knees he had discussed the question with his Intimate Friend: "Lord, if Thou dost want me never to be married, let me know Thy will. But if it be Thy will that I marry, I have one request to make: *help me to find a woman who will love Thee supremely,* for then I am sure she will always love me. Because of her love for Thee, she will put me into the proper place in her affection and devotion. Choose for me, Lord."

Slowly building itself through the years since those times when his mother had hugged him close, told him how happy his father had made her, and said, "Some day my boy will make some little woman unspeakably happy," there had been set up in his mind a standard of what he expected his wife to be. His own pen has described for us the qualities of his ideal:

I came to feel that part of my mission in life, one of the objects of my being, was to make some one little woman happy; while to injure a woman, to mar her life and blast her happiness, seemed to me—and still seems—the supremest cursedness and treason against the most sacred rights and claims of humanity. From mother I unconsciously got a high ideal of gentle sweetness and purity, and all womanly virtues which adorn a home and make it a haven of rest and a center of inspiration and courage and noble ambition.

One of the safeguards of my adolescent years, during those lonely periods after mother died, was the thought of a wife to whom some day I wanted to give myself as pure and unsoiled as I hoped to find her. When tempted to run after forbidden pleasures, that thought was one of the great restraints in my life—one of the supreme protective influences. I wanted so to live that I could open my heart and tell my wife my whole life without shame.

Many years hence, in the reflective years of life's eventide, he penned a brochure on "Why I Wanted My Wife to be My Wife." An extract from this will reveal the mature development of his strict standard:

It was while continuing my professional studies in an Eastern University that the conviction possessed me that my wife must not only have sweet womanly virtues, be adorned with refinement and the culture of the schools, but that she must be genuinely religious, must love God and His law supremely, for without this I realized we should fail in the highest fellowship. But with this love and loyalty we could not fail.

But where could I find such a woman? Solomon was a very wise man and had a very wide marital experience, and he said, "A prudent wife is from the Lord." If she is from the Lord, why not ask Him for her? Why not pray to Him to find her? And this I did.

Thus his almost impossibly high standard. Thus his confident prayer, made as naturally and as expectantly as another would ask for daily bread. But would he get an adequate answer? Would he not have to make qualifying amendments to that standard?

Months and years passed, during which he met many young women of grace, accomplishment, goodness; but none had disturbed his heart or caused him to suspect that she was God's woman for him. Then Elizabeth Swift; a chum hearing her speak, and rushing back to the seminary to say, "Sam, I've found just the girl for you"; and Brengle going to the church, looking upon the little woman clad in Salvation Army uniform, and having feelings which, expressed later, were:

We met, and I fell in love—I lost my heart. Here she was, the sweet, gracious, cultured woman, filled with God's love, one my head and heart approved, and for whose dear sake I had denied myself in lonely hours of fierce temptation (though I had not seen her face), and for whom I had prayed and watched and waited.

Thus his answer, received as instantaneously and with as much finality as though God Himself had sent an angel to lead her by the hand and present her to him.

The revelation that Elizabeth Swift was his God-provided helpmeet, however, had been vouchsafed so far only to him. She regarded him simply as "a brother in Christ," a friend whose ideals were in common with her own, and who was therefore interesting. Opportunity for closer acquaintance came when she invited him to conduct a revival meeting in the church in Amenia, N. Y., where she had, by the use of "Army methods," more than doubled the membership. And, because banker Swift's house was the place where preachers were always entertained, the three weeks Brengle was in Amenia he spent mostly in her company, and with her, "poking about the village, Army fashion."

During this time he led her into conversation upon virtually every topic except love. Their exchanges on the subject of religion were models of candor. Seeing in her spiritual life a lack of joy and communion, he pointed this out to her in a spirit of frankness that ever would characterize their companionship.

She promised to commune more; and in the following week they had additional conversation and correspondence on the matter. But it was not until some time later, when she was resting at a sanatorium in Pennsylvania, that she entered into the experience of which he had told her. She wrote:

You helped me when you showed me that Jesus wanted me for something more than a servant. I had never looked any higher; but I rose higher at the sanatorium; and it was through you I did so, by keeping my promise to pray more in the way of communion and waiting on God. I feel His love about me like sunshine all the while. . . . Ever since He gave me life "more abundantly" I have forgotten more and more my servantship—though that was sweet and dear to me—and have come into the higher life of a friend.

In this manner their friendship ran on: letters, occasional visits, mutual declarations of their faith in God. But, as yet, no declaration of love.

When, however, she was on the eve of departing for England, where she was to spend the winter of 1886-1887 gathering material for a book to be called "The Army Drum," Brengle considered the time ripe for his proposal. The answer he received was as decidedly negative as it was prompt:

You are surely under a spell, an illusion! All my sanctified commonsense says loudly and clearly, "You must *not* marry him!" Some day you will be glad that I couldn't think as you did, that I kept you free. I am *sure* that God means better things for you. Please ask Him, as I do, to set you free.

But he was not interested in praying to be set free from one whom he was so sure God meant for him. He told her so, whereupon she outlined reasons why he must be mistaken: her health was delicate; she was a few years older than he; her father had recently suffered financial reverses and she could hardly think of leaving him; they would be poor, and in time he would have a broken-down old woman on his hands; and so on. After this review of obstacles, there was just this wistful sentiment:

Your proposal has filled me with joy and with intense sadness. I feel that your love, if I could be your wife, would be the crown of my womanhood. But it cannot be.

Undaunted, he persisted, telling her of his prayer, his ideal, God's answer—and how she fitted into all these. None the less, she saw only an unreasoning man in love; even one to whom, perhaps, Satan had presented himself as an angel of light, as witness the following:

I have prayed much and thought much to find out if God meant to give me to you, thinking always in this order—first, of God's will and the good of His cause; next, of your welfare; and last, of the result of my own soul; and I cannot believe that He does mean it. I do not love you except as I would a brother, and when I think of your welfare my very affection for you cries out, "You shall not waste your life so!" Not your love, but your life. God will return that love into your own heart, and some other woman will be blessed with it some day.

And what about my own soul? "A married woman careth for the things of this world, that she may please her husband." I am sure that I should get worldly, and be always thinking how to look young and as nearly pretty as I could, just to please you. I should *surely* in that way put you before God, and I dare not risk that.

You say that your life must be one of utter devotion to the Man Christ Jesus? How that fills my soul with joy. I cannot ever risk hindering that.

Did ever woman marshal such arguments—arguments that so militated against her own heart happiness? Resolutely, and with cold logic which she would not give her heart a chance to melt, she put from her all thoughts of him whom many a woman would have considered a rare "catch."

And there the matter stood when she sailed. As for her, she considered the question closed, and in England went about her work, traveling, interviewing, writing—feeling confident that the months of their separation would be sufficient to disillusion the young preacher.

In the meantime Brengle had given himself to other thoughts as well as to those of her. Chief among these was the question whether he would follow what he had for many months recognized as God's leading, and offer himself as a candidate for officership in The Salvation Army. This he met with characteristic thoroughness and expedition.

Hence, upon Elizabeth Swift's return to America, when he repeated with renewed ardor his proposal, he could do so armed with the not inconsequential argument of his recent decision. This time, her absence having proved to her that her regard for him ran deeper than a mere feeling of brotherly love, she did not so tersely refuse him consideration. "Give me time to pray about it," she said. And two days later he returned to hear her decision: "It is all right. I feel He has chosen for me. It is His will. And He has given me this text: 'He shall choose our inheritance for us.' "

Days of exquisite happiness followed, days filled with eager discussion of plans for their future. When they came to debate the question of his training for officership, however, an awkward angle protruded itself. They had agreed that, for the purpose of his proper inoculation with the Army spirit and in order for him to study at first hand the workings of The Army, a period of training was to be desired; but as there was as yet no Training Garrison in the United States, it was plain that this would mean a lengthy separation. They settled the problem in a manner that was to become characteristic of them: It was decided that they should be married first—the date was set for May 19th of that year, 1887—following which he would sail for London to be trained at Clapton Training Garrison.

Many, faced with the same sacrifice, would have fore-gone training, or given up their calling altogether. Not so this couple. They began their life together with the practice of a slogan that henceforth was always to govern it: *"God first!"*

Their love fast came into flower. If, in the days of his unspoken courtship, Brengle might have thought Lily cold, unresponsive, incapable of deep affection, such thoughts now were forever dispelled. Her love, pent-up and awaiting the man who could win her heart, now gushed forth like a spring just released from winter's snows.

When all preparations for the wedding had been made, and he had returned to Boston to wind up his affairs as an evangelist, she wrote:

Since I can't slip away into the north room and pray with you this morning, I must write and tell you how I'd like to. God keeps me in perfect peace and rest, and doesn't let me miss you. . . . All the same I'd love to have you here this morning. It rests me more than anything else to put my head on your shoulder and my hand in yours. I used to think that a lover would take my thoughts away from God, but you do not; you draw me nearer to him. God bless you!

I was tempted for a while yesterday to think that perhaps we should not be married *now*. But after praying it all seemed quite clear, and I am sure that it is best for the Kingdom. And now I am perfectly contented, resting, quite happy.

She was writing to him every day now. "Awfully silly, isn't it? I've always said so!" Nevertheless, she indulged herself in this bit of silliness just the same.

Hearing that in Boston he, for the first time as a Salvationist, was taking an active part in Salvation Army meetings, and in so doing was experiencing persecution, she wrote, glorying in his shame-suffering:

I'm glad you don't mind being hooted for doing God's work. You simply won't hear them shout after a while, or, if you do, it will only make you feel happy and glad. I shall never like to have you abused, dear, but I shall be glad that you are counted worthy to suffer shame for His name!

I want to be your comfort, your help. I *must* share all your sorrows, though I'd like you to have *all* the joy. I'd far rather know of any trouble that happens to you than of any pleasant thing that comes to you. You will take me into your "dark chambers," won't you, my Sam?

Two days before the wedding, he was in Amenia, and as the time for their long separation drew nearer, bringing its pang in the midst of her happiness, she took advantage of his temporary absence from the house to write him a letter which she would enclose in an envelope marked "To be delivered Thursday, May 26," when he would be on board ship sailing for London:

Sam, my dearest, you're at the meeting now, and I've just been up in your room to put a steamer bag in your drawer, and stopped to pray for you. I knelt by the bedside, where it looked as though you had been kneeling before me, and gave you over to God. I didn't like to think of you ill, and worn out, and going away from me, and so I had to put you into Father's hands again. I *can* leave you there.

Isn't it glorious, my Sam, when we think of the miles of water that must soon separate us, to remember that "neither height, nor depth, nor any other creature can separate us from the love of Christ"—and in that love we can always meet!

May 19th arrived. The library of the Swift home, where the wedding was to take place, was banked with apple blossoms from the orchards; in the air was the delicate fragrance of lilies-of-the-valley. When the guests came, they were found to include most of the local aristocracy, since the Swifts were members of society's upper crust. These, however, were decidedly in the minority, for in the push and jostle of the crowd making its way through the front gate were the community's commonalty: the poor of the township, Lily's converts, attendants at her little meetings, farm hands, kitchen girls.

The ceremony itself was beautiful in its simplicity, and followed the form of the Salvation Army Marriage Service. While a tone of gladness and joy pervaded the atmosphere, "first things" were not forgotten even in this happy hour: afterwards both Sam and Lily gave their testimonies and exhorted their guests to give themselves as completely to God as they, the bride and groom, had given themselves to each other.

Two days later, on the morning of the day his ship was to sail, Lily was sitting in their hotel room in New York City, the terminus of their short wedding trip. While he was downstairs bidding a few friends farewell, she wrote him a short note which she hid in his pocket:

My dearest, I asked God on the train today for some word straight from Him, for my own soul alone—which, if I needed a lesson, should shut even you out. But He gave me the old: "Have faith in God." Bless His name! I *will* have faith in Him—I do just now. I'm glad to give you to Him for a while, knowing He will surely give you back to me.

Down at the wharf, a few hours later, the boat whistle blew. Goodbyes were said. And he was off for London and the Training Garrison.

The next day, when the folds of her loneliness and the realization of her sacrifice had enwrapped her, Lily consoled herself by writing Sam a long letter. Here is one paragraph:

Every once in a while it flashes across me that, with every beat of my heart, that remorseless propeller is pushing you across the water farther and farther away from me. The consciousness comes

as a sudden laugh from the Devil. I don't entertain it—I can't.
Darling, people think I am a hard-hearted wretch to let you go, but
I'm not. I'm not! *You* know it, my Sam. Outside people can't
understand any of it—but we two inside people can. Lord, keep
me from ever getting where I can't give up my sweetheart for
Thee!

Chapter VIII

CADET

On june 1, 1887, at The Army's International Headquarters in London, two men sat in an office, facing each other. Twinkling hazel eyes of Samuel Logan Brengle, twenty-seven, looked deep into piercing grey eyes of William Booth, fifty-eight.

"General, I have come."

A moment of silence. No handclasp, no warm words of welcome. An observer would have remarked that the General surveyed his candidate rather coldly, seeing the latter had dropped a promising ministry and had come 3,000 miles to give himself to The Salvation Army. Finally the General spoke:

"Brengle, you belong to the dangerous classes. You have been your own boss for so long that I don't think you will want to submit to Salvation Army discipline. We are an Army, and we demand obedience."

"Well, General, I have received the Holy Spirit as my Sanctifier and Guide. I feel He has led me to offer myself to you. Give me a chance."

After this manner did they thrust and parry—the cultured young preacher of the schools and the gruff and fiery apostle of the world's down-trodden. Two days later, Brengle, in a letter to his bride, described the remainder of the interview:

He quoted Scripture to me, paternally advised me not to take any vows upon myself hastily, assuring me that The Army presented

72

only a field for hard work and self-denial, and that the greatest of all must become the servants of all. I managed to get in a few words "edgeways," told him I had never sought a place but once, and that was before I entered the ministry at all, that I knew my only way up to Heaven was by going down to the lowest of the low, and that I wanted to go. That seemed to inspire him with some confidence that I was not wholly dangerous, and, grasping my hand, he said, "God bless you!" He then advised me to see the Chief [Bramwell Booth] soon, invited me to the "all night of prayer" at the Congress Hall, and kindly dismissed me. I love him. He's a dear old man.

Meanwhile, he had acquired his first uniform. A description of it, and of his reactions before first appearing in it in public, went into a letter to Lily:

You should see me in uniform! Susie and Frances [his sister-in-law and a friend] grow jubilant over it, and Susie maintains that a man's only half a man till he gets under the cap. Well, I am *proud*, in a proper sense, of it. But—I—half—way—dread—going out for the first time with it on. I am not used to being stared at so curiously. But I shall trust the Lord to shut me in with Himself and not let me feel, nor care for, what man can do unto me.

When finally he was able to see the Chief of the Staff, he was at first received with scarcely more enthusiasm than that which had been displayed by the General. Again he was told he belonged to "the dangerous classes" (evidently a stock phrase for describing candidates of his type), with the added prediction: "You will probably stay with us for a year or two, and then you will get out. In that case, you will have just lost all that time. Really, we think you might as well stay out."

Finally, however, when the Chief saw that his enthusiastic candidate was not even remotely interested in the suggestion that he should "stay out," he agreed to give him a trial, sending him to Leamington, one of the field-training depots where cadets were given part of their instruction.

At Leamington he expected to enter at once upon a continuous round of soul-saving work. He was hardly prepared for the blow to his illusions which came when he was assigned to his first duty: he was told to black the boots of the other cadets! See him:

Down in the dark little cellar he found himself with eighteen pairs of muddy shoes, a can of blacking, and a sharp temptation. It was not the lowliness of the duty but the apparent waste of his time and talent that had wounded him. Remembering his Lord's story of the man who buried his talent, he prayed, the while his brush moved inexpertly across the toe of a clumsy boot: "Lord God, am I burying my talent? Is this the best they can do for me in The Salvation Army? Am I a fool? Have I followed my own fancy 3,000 miles to come here to black boots?"

As if in direct answer, in imagination he saw a picture: Jesus was the central figure, and He was washing the disciples' feet! His Lord—Who had come from the bosom of the Everlasting Father and the glories of Heaven and the adoration of its hosts—bending over the feet of uncouth, unlearned fishermen, washing them, humbling Himself, taking the form of a servant!

In the light of this revelation, Brengle's heart was bowed low: "Dear Lord, Thou didst wash their feet; I will black their boots!" And with an enthusiasm heretofore unknown to the boot-blacking profession, he tackled his job, a song on his lips, peace in his heart.

Years later he would say:

I had fellowship with Jesus every morning for a week while down in that cellar blacking boots. It was the best training I could have had. I was humble, but now I was practising my humility. I saw what The Salvation Army stood for—service. My new prayer was, "Dear Lord, let me serve the servants of Jesus. That is sufficient for me." And, do you know, that experience put a key in my hand to unlock the hearts of lowly people all round the world!

Having caught the swing of the depot routine, he enjoyed the activity and his share of the inconveniences. Writing home, he said jubilantly: "Your lad is at last in active service. 'Roughing it,' glory to God!"

Never having tried to march before, he found it difficult to pick up and put down his feet in rhythm with the drum, and laughed at his awkwardness on the march. Because the quarters were small and cramped, with not room in the dining room for all the cadets at once, he gave another his place at the table, and ate his morning bowl of porridge off the bottom of an overturned tub in the tiny courtyard outside. There were meetings every night, and on Sundays frequently as many as seven in which he took part. Between meetings he sold *War Crys* and engaged in visitation, both of which tasks appealed to him as not only novel but delightful and profitable.

As his experience and ability became revealed, he was used frequently as a "special." But the more he was thus used, the closer was the watch he put over his own heart. An old temptation made its appearance:

I find Satan tempting me to seek rapid promotion—it's on the lines of my old ecclesiastical ambitions. Dear Lord, save me from it. Would you be disappointed very much, my sweet wife, if I should take a low rank in The Army? I want to be useful. God save me from wanting to be famous. He does save me from it, bless His name.

It happened that on the fourth anniversary of his graduation from DePauw, he was called upon to relate his lifestory. An excerpt from a letter written the next day in-

dicates how he now regarded the path into which he had
been led thus far:

Last night the Captain had me tell my experience. It was the
fourth anniversary of my graduation from college—a strange coin-
cidence. How little I then thought of the marvellous way God
would lead me! I'm glad He veiled the future, for I should certainly have drawn back and gone to perdition, but following Him
step by step He has at last led me down, down, to where I can
rejoice in humiliation, seeking not my own but our heavenly Father's
pleasure, desiring not my own but His glory.

That very early in his Army career Brengle sensed what
was to be his particular field of service is seen in a letter
which he wrote to Mrs. Brengle on June 20, 1887, when he
had been a Salvationist less than two months and a cadet
hardly more than a fortnight:

I don't know yet, of course, what kind of a little place God has for
us in The Army, but I feel that my work will be particularly to
promote holiness. I should like to be a Special to go about and hold
half-nights of prayer just to lead people into the experience of
holiness.

A month later, when he had been taken from the Leamington depot and was being used in the very capacity which
he predicted for himself, he wrote:

I find that my work is to be principally with soldiers and officers.
Staff-Captain tells me this morning that I am to do considerable
work in his district and that he wants me to do nothing but conduct
holiness meetings. Glory to God! How I do thank the dear Lord
that He is opening the way for me to do this work. Just the work I
would choose. O Lord, give me wisdom, love, and the fulness of
the Spirit! I sometimes wonder if God means me for a kind of
holiness evangelist to The Army. . . . !

It is notable also, that though his vision here of his
future place in The Army was new, it was by no means

narrow. Mark the import of the underscored phrase "the whole Army":

Pray much for me, that I may be used to quicken the spiritual life of *the whole Army.* I want to be so definite and so burning that God will be manifested wherever I go. I am not anxious for place or name, and if God can use me to glorify Him just as well at the rear as at the front, I shall gladly say, Amen. I have been led from the beginning to pray that I might be a blessing, not simply to some little corps, but to *the whole* Army. I say *led,* God has led me thus to pray, and I believe He will answer, but I do not anticipate that in answering He will necessarily give me some prominent place where everybody can see me. *On the contrary, I see that He can easily answer that prayer and yet keep me in obscurity, and if He so chooses I shall rejoice.*

For six weeks he was engaged with these special meetings, visiting, among other corps and training stations, in Leighton, Kettering, London, Northampton, Wellingboro, Oxford, Banbury. For the most part his work was attended by unusual results: many were converted, many sanctified. Following these he was appointed, as part of his preliminary work, to take charge of Stamford Corps for a month. Then back to Clapton.

Out on the field, in the depots, and on the platform as he had been engaged in leading meetings, his superior officers had kept an eye on him. Now, as he came to Clapton, what sort of specialized training did they see he needed? One weakness, apparently, was his "long-winded-ness." He had been told that he was to "spend some time with the Booths and others, who are to take me in hand and train me to be *brief* and 'Blood-and-Fire'."

Another shortcoming was his lack of business and organizing ability. Never having been in an executive position, never having had to handle underlings, control finance, make up books, he had this lack, felt it, admitted it. Yet he had no taste for these things. One day, after having taken an objective look at himself, he let his pen say:

Just when I'll return to America is uncertain. I think the uncertainty all arises from my utter lack of business tact and training—they don't know where to put me. If I had business qualifications, they'd make a D. C. of me at once, but not considering that expedient, they are waiting to find a place for me. Well, inasmuch as I am *not* a business man, and have no such phrenological bump as encourages me to ever hope to be, I'm going to draw comfort from Acts 6:24. I know God has a place or me. I think He saw that I would be in the S. A. and it is highly probable that He had somewhat to do with my training for the work.

Looking forward to his return to America, he felt a passion for the salvation and blessing of the people of his native land take hold of him:

He filled my heart with a burning desire for America. O such desire! I see it now. My desire to return has heretofore been in large measure selfish—not so much for His perishing sheep as for you, my darling. This morning he has put prayer in my mouth and in my heart for America. My whole heart longs for the dear people there, to help them, to stir them up, to pray with them and for them, and above all to insist upon holiness of heart and life among them. That's my work. Wherever I am placed, in whatever part of the field, that is the one thing God asks me to do.

"To insist upon holiness. . . . That is the one thing!" See here a man of one idea, one thought, one passion! Many years later his comrade officers were to look at him and his powerful ministry and wonder what was his secret. Then they would trace back through the decades and find it, strongly evidenced, in his very first days with The Army: One passion—holiness: for himself, for The Army, for the whole world of professed followers of the holy Son of God.

With such a spirit he worked, prayed, preached,

marched, listened to lectures, scrubbed floors, visited, sold *War Crys*—taking advantage of every experience, every opportunity, that would help to mold him into a Salvationist of the Blood-and-Fire stamp.

The final two days of the training session were devoted to anniversary meetings commemorating the founding of the Training Garrison, and led by the General, William Booth.

After the final meeting, Brengle sought out the General for a word of farewell.

"May I say goodbye, General? I am sailing tomorrow for America."

"Oh, so soon? Come with me."

Going to a little room back of the platform, they sat together for a half hour, the General telling of his most fervent hopes for The Salvation Army. They prayed in turn, and when Brengle went through the door, the General put his arms about him, kissed him, and said, "Be kind to my boy.* He is only a young man." In days to come, Brengle was to have cause to remember that loving injunction, and be kind—"for his father's sake."

Thus intimate had these two become—the General and Founder of the fast-spreading Salvation Army and the young man whom, only six months ago, he had tried to discourage because he belonged to "the dangerous classes."

Time would continue to tell just how "dangerous" was Brengle to The Salvation Army.

---

* Ballington, who at this time was Commander-in-Chief of the U. S. forces.

Chapter IX

CORPS OFFICER

In the first nine months of his officership—from December, 1887, to September, 1888—Captain Brengle had command of three corps: Taunton, Massachusetts, and South Manchester and Danbury, Connecticut. Measured by the standards for corps in America at that time, they represented the worst, the best, and the neither worst nor best—in reverse of the order named. Due to the short stay system then generally in vogue, he could do scarcely more than a surface work at any of these appointments. It is interesting, nevertheless, to observe how he handled the various problems presented by each. He was no genius of versatility; he had but one method for all problems requiring solution. Watching that method, we shall see the man.

Arriving in Taunton, Brengle found The Army there to be, at least on the surface, a fair example of the average small-town corps: twenty soldiers, a few brass instruments, a hall that would seat between 300 and 400 people, and an audience that averaged about 100.

Characteristically, he was not content with the surface appearance of things. The question paramount in his mind as he looked over his little flock was not, "How many do we have here?" but, "What kind of soldiers have we here?" Probing their spiritual experience he was no little chagrined to find only one of the twenty professed to be sanctified. This he considered a deplorable state of affairs, and resolved at once that before going out to do battle against sinners he would either properly equip or summarily dispense with the members of his fighting force.

If the mental picture that we get of Captain Brengle at this time is that of a too strict preceptor of holiness, firmly clutching his yardstick, prepared to measure without leniency all claimants to spirituality, he must not be too harshly judged, since the error is one to which youthful earnestness is ever prone. When a few more years had given him broader wisdom with men and God he said: "I'm afraid I was not always wise in those early days. I expected too much from those poor soldiers. It was like giving mature wisdom to a child, expecting him to take it in, or like giving strong meat to a babe, and expecting him to digest it."

At this point, however, he saw in his soldiers' lack of the holiness experience both an explanation of the corps' present poverty and a certain prophecy of disaster to come. He determined, therefore, to make holiness the issue. Properly presented, it would operate sharply upon the soldiers' hearts, dividing the consecrated and sanctified from the holding-back and unsanctified, with the hope that the latter would either be driven on and up, or out and away. If they could not be mended, it would be better if their connection with the corps were ended.

Affairs during the following three months took on a healthy complexion. Mrs. Brengle joined him, and together they held meetings, visited, prayed and worked, making Taunton hum with Salvation Army activity. At the expiration of that happy time, however, Mrs. Brengle was taken ill and had to return to Amenia, and almost immediately a long line of dour-faced trials put in their appearance.

First, the corps, because of an unfriendly landlord, was put out of its hall; attempts to get another proving vain, the little army of soldiers were forced to take to the street for all their public meetings, the quarters being made to serve as an indoor meeting-place for knee-drills, holiness and soldiers' meetings. Added to this inconvenience, financial troubles arose: no salary was forthcoming, and the payments on the rent for the quarters went long overdue.

Internal difficulties also came. Originating with those soldiers who had refused to come up to the high standard Captain Brengle had set up, petty envyings, jealousies, and strife made things unpleasant. Then, to add to these trials, scarlet fever broke out, and the quarters were quarantined for two weeks. During the enforced inactivity of this period, fresh temptations assailed him from every side. Yet through all these testings he manifested a buoyant spirit. Here was no sulking prophet under a juniper tree, no disconsolate Job in a bed of ashes. In his diary he wrote a passage reflecting serenity amid cloudy circumstances:

I'm like a thirsty Arab following a mirage. My hopes are suddenly lifted high and then dashed to the ground. But, glory to God! My faith holds like an anchor. His grace is sufficient!

When, after five months, he farewelled from Taunton, it was not with regrets for duty half performed, but with a feeling that he had "declared the whole counsel of God," and that though some might have counted his work a failure, he himself was not afraid of the Eternal check-up:

I have done what I could. I have held up Christ. I have ploughed and planted and watered the seed with my tears and God has given me a few sheaves. I feel that my soul is clear of the blood of all men. Somehow I rest. Never did a prophet feel more free when his message was delivered than do I. Bless God forever!

A very different type of corps was South Manchester. His appointment here was pro tem, he having been sent to "hold on" for three weeks while the officer was on furlough. His first impressions were:

South Manchester is, I think, the prettiest town I ever saw, and I believe this is about the best corps I ever saw. More than sixty soldiers were in the march yesterday; it was a sight to see them. Most of the women had on plain blue dresses, and most of the men were in uniform, so that it was really a beautiful sight. They are a nice-looking lot—most all North of Ireland people, and a few Germans.

Pleased as he was, however, at the sight of much uniform, a stirring march, and many soldiers, these outward signs of prosperity did not keep him from looking deeper. And beneath the surface of things he saw a gap between perfection of organization and perfection of spiritual life:

They need holiness very much. Some of them have stood just about as long as they can stand without it. I think I can see how some of them have begun to lose power through the lack of it. I trust God has sent me just in time, to show them the "missing link."

Therefore, with his time here so short, was it not his most important duty, and the one that should prove of the most lasting worth, to get the soldiers sanctified?

As I have but a short time to stay, I would much rather spend it in getting the soldiers sanctified and filled with the Holy Ghost, than to try to get sinners saved. I am not indifferent to sinners—God forbid! But my heart yearns for the soldiers, that they may be "rooted and grounded in love" and established in the faith.

Further, he was convinced that—

The shout of hallelujahs and the noise of tamborines won't feed the soul, nor will stirring appeals to sinners six nights out of the week, and scathing anathemas against tobacco and bustles the seventh night, build up soldiers and make them robust men in Christ. They need "the sincere milk of the Word."

The results of Brengle's emphasis on holiness in South Manchester were such that they will live as long as the memories of those soldiers survive. With but few exceptions, the entire soldiery of the corps were sanctified during his stay, among them being the present Colonel Joseph Atkinson,* who dates his "establishing" from this time. Another result of his stay here was a new rule adopted by the band, stating that no man might play in or be a member of the band unless he professed and possessed the Blessing of a Clean Heart.

* * *

But like moving from green pasture to arid desert was his going from South Manchester to Danbury.

Since Mrs. Brengle, at home in Amenia where she was preparing to welcome their first child, was unable to come to help him, he went on to Danbury alone. He found the corps considerably in debt; his only assistant a lame Lieutenant; no soldiers at all upon whom he could depend for help, save a huge Negro named George Washington and a little hunchback girl; a miserable quarters of four small, hot and stuffy rooms, barely furnished; and stacks of unsold and unpaid-for *War Crys*. Even more disheartening was the discovery that he had come on the heels of a nauseous scandal which had made almost impossible the getting of either crowds or financial support.

Despite the fact that Danbury was, in many respects, a tougher proposition than Taunton, there are not to be found in his Danbury letters the records of any such soul struggles as those detailed in his Taunton letters. It is as though in the strenuous conflicts of Taunton he had won

---

* Provincial Commander, New England, U. S. A.

victories that now stood him in good stead at Danbury. With a spirit only rarely downcast, he faced the debts and the scandal, marched the streets with his big Negro and little hunchback, lived jubilantly in his stuffy little quarters, and went about the business of corps building with holy vim and verve.

And gradually his faith and persistence began to bear fruit: attendance at the meetings increased, sinners were saved, soldiers were enrolled. On August 10, 1888, two months after he had taken charge, he could write:

> We had eleven in the open-air ring night before last. Glory to God! The largest number yet. Our crowds have been good this week, not fewer than fifty any night, and most interesting open-airs. The Lord is surely working on the hearts of the people, and we will reap the fruits of our labors.

He was, nevertheless, not without temptation to compare his present position with that in which he might have been. One night, when marching down the street with his lame Lieutenant, the big Negro, and the little hunchback girl, his voice and theirs lifted bravely in the song "We're The Army That Shall Conquer!" he came suddenly abreast a large and imposing Methodist Church. His glance swept across the broad front and traveled upward to the tall spire; the great church seemed to look down upon him and his little flock with infinite condescension and derision. And immediately a mocking voice broke out across the song to smite him in the heart: "You fool, you! You might have been the pastor of a great church like that. But here you are instead, the pastor of a big Negro and a little hunchback!" For a moment his voice faltered in the ambitious assertion concerning his "conquering" Army, and he was inclined to agree with his tempter. Only for a moment, however. In the next he had remembered all God's dealings with him, and, turning his eyes back to his pitifully small group, smiled to them with encouragement and pride, swung his arm vigorously and was leading them again in "We're The Army That Shall Conquer!"

When he farewelled, after three and a half months of labor in Danbury, and went to Mrs. Brengle at Amenia, he could feel that he had achieved his desire for the blessing of the people as he had outlined it in a letter on his first day in Danbury:

I do want these people blessed . . . and when I say "blessed" I don't mean "made a little better," but convicted, condemned and crucified—and then resurrected in Christ to a new and holy life that doesn't feed on noise and bluster and parade, but that lives on hidden manna, bread that the world knows not of.

* * *

You are appointed as officer-in-charge of Boston Number 1 corps."

Captain Brengle, seated at the table one morning in November, 1888, read this message on a telegram. Going over the words again, he experienced a feeling of faintness, and when Mrs. Brengle placed food before him, he said, simply, "Darling, I have no appetite." Boston 1 corps! Though he had always held himself ready for any appointment, the possibility of being sent to Boston, and especially to this particular corps in that city, had never before occurred o him.

He knew Boston 1. He had frequently attended meetings there before he joined The Army. Memories of the place now crowded in upon him: the Army building, located on a narrow, noisy side street in a Negro quarter of the West End; just across from the hall, one of the most disreputable saloons in the city; upstairs, the quarters, scarcely better than a hovel.

Another fact that helped to make the appointment appear a living martyrdom was that in Boston he had a wide circle of friends and acquaintances, many of whom he would be bound to meet, some of whom doubtless would come to his meetings, see his poverty, think how the mighty had fallen, and either sniff superiorly or pity condescendingly—one as bad as the other. Boston 1, therefore, stood for a Calvary for which he had not prepared.

Small wonder his appetite left him!

Even so, these thoughts had no sooner visited him than he felt ashamed. Casting aside any thought of self-loss, he probed immediately for the cause of his vagrant feelings:

"Lord, why do I feel this way? Am I proud? Is this appointment an offense to that pride? Am I not dead to these things?" As though in response there came to his mind the words of the Apostle Paul, who, when his friends entreated him not to return to Jerusalem lest he be bound and thrown into prison, had replied: "What mean ye to weep and to break my heart? For I am ready not to be bound only, but also to die at Jerusalem for the name of the Lord Jesus."

That was enough. "Dear Lord," said Brengle, "I too will be faithful. I am willing not only to go to Boston, and to suffer there if necessary, but I am willing even to die in Boston for Thee!" Instantly his appetite returned and he ate heartily. Little did he then know, however, just how near to dying for Christ he was to come.

To Boston, accordingly, the Brengles went. In that cramped, squalid quarters they lived. From that saloon across the street, night after night, came sodden hordes of drunkards to crowd the little hall, start drunken bouts, break up the seats and the services.

But meetings in which drunks figured so prominently and riotously were not the only gatherings held in that little hall. There were soldiers' meetings, blessed times, of which Brengle said when writing one day, years later, to a young officer:

In my soldiers' meetings, I dealt very promptly with any business that we had on hand, and then we had a Bible reading and a red-hot prayer meeting, and the soldiers got so blessed that outsiders used to beg to come in.

Another feature were the all-day holiness meetings conducted monthly at the corps. These were attended by Salvationists from all the Boston corps and from nearby cities, and also attracted many church people who came to look upon the corps as a Delphi of the higher life. Of these meetings, Malcolm Salmond,* at that time a soldier of the Boston 1 corps, would write forty-two years later:

With all its poverty, that little upstairs hall during the stay of Captain and Mrs. Brengle was the Mecca of many of the greatest teachers and preachers of holiness that New England then possessed. Once a month they met there for a holiness gathering; and as I look back I can see many of those illustrious men and women, their garments soiled from kneeling on the plain board floor stained by the tread of a thousand sinners' feet. The poor and illiterate, too, helped to crowd these meetings. Hundreds of those who attended have since passed on, but many an officer and soldier and Christian friend can date the beginning of his higher religious experience from those days.

In the midst of his mingled struggles and victories at Boston 1 Corps, there came the incident that cut short his career as a corps officer, and, indeed, very nearly finished him for a career of any kind:

---

* Staff-Captain Salmond (R).

Entering the long, narrow hallway which led to the stairway and hall upstairs, Brengle one evening discovered a "tough" who had come over from the saloon across the street and was comporting himself in an unseemly manner. Having asked the man to get out, and meeting with only insolence and attempted violence in return, Brengle gently but firmly ushered him through the door. The ejected one, however, waited his revenge, and when Brengle appeared again in the doorway he hurled a whole paving brick at his ejector. Since the man was not more than ten feet away at the time, the brick struck Brengle's head full force, smashing it against the door post.

For days Brengle hovered between life and death; then, rallying, he was packed off to a health resort in New York State for treatment. There he remained for six weeks, returning at the end of that period to Amenia, where he was compelled to forego active service for a further period of eighteen months.

During this time he was not altogether inactive. When the condition of his injury would allow, he devoted his time to writing articles for *The War Cry* and other Army publications. These articles were later collected into a little book dealing with the higher life, with the title "Helps to Holiness," which had a phenomenal sale, many editions being published in many lands. It went around the world in a dozen Occidental and Oriental languages. When anyone would mention to its author how much blessing they had received from the book, Brengle would smile and say, "Well, if there had been no little brick, there would have been no little book!"

After returning from the health resort, Brengle one day found his wife painting a text on the brick. She had kept it, saying that she intended making a collection of all the bricks with which her husband would be knocked down.

The text she had chosen was that word from Joseph to his brethren who had sold him into Egypt: "As for you, ye meant it for evil; but God meant it for good to keep much people alive."

Recovering sufficiently to conduct a meeting now and then, Brengle was importuned to return for an all-day holiness meeting at Boston 1 corps. Here he was accosted by the new Divisional Commander, whom he had not met till now: "One of the reasons I wanted to come to this command was to see you, Captain Brengle. I have read your articles, and wanted to get acquainted with you. Couldn't you do some meetings for us: work a day and rest a day, or work a day and rest a week, or work a day and rest a month, if necessary—but do something to help us, by going about conducting meetings in our corps." To this Brengle agreed.

While on his tour of this Division, he entered into a new kind of covenant with God: *a consecration for failure.* It came about in the following way:

Considering what this campaign might mean in the way of future appointments, the thought had come to him: "The Commander will be watching you now, sizing up your work, judging your abilities; you'd better make good." He recognized at once, however, the evil behind that attitude, and prayed: "Lord, take away this restlessness and fear of what men may think or do," then added this covenant: "I am willing, Lord, to go around this division and preach holiness and salvation to the very best of my ability. But if I don't see a tear shed, a sinner saved, a backslider reclaimed, or a Christian sanctified, I will still rejoice in Thee!" His first two appointments were full of spiritual blessing, many people seeking the Lord; but his third appointment turned out to be difficult. Thereupon, when no response was made to his appeals and he was tempted to open the door to his old depression, he remembered his covenant, rejoiced in spite of drought, and the next day saw a great break in the ranks of evil.

Promotion to the rank of Adjutant came. And shortly afterward, he received an appointment as District Officer for Maine and New Hampshire. This put his corps officer days forever in the past.

CHAPTER X

DISTRICT AND PROVINCIAL OFFICER

BRENGLE began his work as a District Officer with faith and flourish. His letters, written at this time in an unusually large and hurried scrawl, reflect the breathlessness of a man entering with rush and relish upon new work. He traveled much, conducting meetings, inspecting corps, dealing with his officers. Sleep became only a necessary evil: he found it impossible to get to bed before midnight, and imperative that he get up no later than 4:30 A. M.

In the District he discovered little to encourage him; his friends, writing, offered their condolences as to one who had been given "the toughest nut of a District in America." Mrs. Brengle received this letter from him:

We are in a dreadful way, darling. My heart is heavy. I don't know which way to turn. Jesus alone knows what I am to do for officers. I am confronted with piles of correspondence, meetings, deserted corps, sick officers, perplexed and disheartened soldiers, poor finances, as well as my care for you.

Yet, despite these and many other difficulties rising before him, notice in the following his place of emphasis; his heart is crying to God for a revival!

I do long to see just such times all over Maine and N. H. My heart is crying to God for a general revival and baptisms of the Holy Ghost and fire all over the District. Pray for it, darling. The Lord must want it more than I do, and in answer to prayer He will give it!

Expressions such as the above are not isolated; his letters covering this period abound with similar passages. Business and finance, if mentioned at all, are mentioned only casually. He gloried not in statistics, but in "a wonderful meeting last night!"

Let it not be thought, however, that he was an impractical mystic, withdrawing himself in holy disdain from the necessity of gathering filthy lucre, leaving to his hapless officers the burden of paying his way about. Often, while visiting poor corps, he would take a few hours from the day for soliciting, raise more than enough to pay the expense of his visit, then refuse to accept anything for his own traveling needs.

Such a policy, however, frequently necessitated his cutting to the very bone his traveling budget. Often, sitting up all night in a dusty day coach, and having not even enough money to buy a meal, he would purchase a five-cent pop-corn ball, munch that, and be satisfied in soul if not in body.

In his relation to his officers and soldiers, he conceived his role as that of a shepherd; he was not their superior, but their servant. Because he thus took his pattern from not man but Christ, his leadership was Christian leadership personified. There were, of course, those who criticized him as "soft," "too easy," "not enough wrist," and so on. But who among them knew so well as he how to influence those he led through love and spiritual imagination rather than through a sense of duty and obedience to authority?

"We must go in more than ever to bless and strengthen our officers; let us plan and pray for this!" is an oft-recurring sentiment appearing in his letters to Mrs. Brengle. Here is another in the same tenor, a shrewd observation on what could, if allowed to do so, become a killing fault in any organization:

> We [officers of The Army] preach a few fundamentals, but we seem so wrapped up in the "work" and so bent on "organization" that there is not that earnest digging after "things old and new" with which to feed the faith, enliven the hope, and inflame the love of our people. The Lord stir us up and help us to "feed the flock which He has purchased with His own Blood!" Oh, for more teachers among us! Leaders who know how to read hearts and apply truth to the needs of the people as a good physician reads his patients and applies remedies to their ills. There are soul-sicknesses open and obscure, acute and chronic, superficial and deep-seated, which the truth as it is in Christ Jesus will heal, but it is not the same truth for each need, any more than the same medicine for each disease. That is why we should most diligently study the Bible and pray for the constant and powerful illumination of the Spirit.

In his personal dealings with his officers the order always was: first the man, then his work. One officer recalls this:

> His first question, upon visiting our corps, and when we were alone together, was "How are you in your own soul, Captain? In the midst of your responsibilities, are you keeping close to God and allowing the Heavenly Father to pour His love afresh in your heart so that you are fit to deal with your soldiers and the poor lost souls of dying men?" And following such questions we would pray, his arm about my shoulders, his voice talking to God in that intimate, conversational way of his. Let me tell you, I would arise from such a season of helpful prayer with a feeling that I'd rather die and be lost than have him find me lax, either in my own experience or in my corps work!

On May 22, 1895, after two and a half years in the Maine and New Hampshire District, Brengle was farewelled and appointed to succeed Staff-Captain Stephen Marshall as District Officer for the Western Massachusetts and Rhode Island District, with headquarters at Worcester. With the transfer came his promotion to the rank of Staff-Captain.

A reporter from the Worcester *Spy,* calling for an interview on July 5, 1895, described Brengle for the readers of his paper:

> The Staff-Captain is a slightly built man with handsome black beard and a face whose striking characteristics are its extreme pallor and the mildness of its expression. He has a high, broad forehead that speaks of intellect and veneration, and his voice is that of one who speaks with the earnestness of his convictions. His whole bearing is that of a man who has struggled long and hard in the fight . . . and who is still struggling.

His stay in the Western Massachusetts and Rhode Island District covered a period of about a year, during which he repeated the successes, the sacrifices, and the increased elevation of the spiritual tone of his command which marked his term in Maine and New Hampshire.

In April, 1896, his work here was terminated only because of a national calamity that befell The Salvation Army in America, rocking the organization to its foundations, and threatening entire disruption. In the "healing of the breaches" he was to play a most important part.

* * *

"BREAK IN SALVATIONISTS' RANKS!" shouted a prominent headline in the Chicago *Record.* "BALLINGTON BOOTHS HAVE WITHDRAWN; MAY DIVIDE SALVATION ARMY" declared bold type on the front page of the New York *Times.*

Pacing the floor of his stateroom on board a ship hurrying him back to London from India, was General William Booth, pulling his long beard and saying, eyes moist and jaw set, that The Army is one, its discipline is one, and that no exceptions shall be made to the rules governing the farewell of officers, and especially not so for officer members of his own family. At his desk at International Headquarters in London sat Bramwell Booth, Chief of the Staff, dictating a cable to "My Dear Comrades of America," which included these sentences:

A great calamity has fallen upon you, and a great sorrow upon The Army everywhere. . . . Your late beloved and honored Commanders have refused to obey the General's orders, and have resigned. . . . In this day of stern trial I call upon you to stand fast to God, to the world-wide purpose of The Army, and to the Flag. Be ready to suffer for the principles you have espoused.

Out in the hinterland of the Salvation Army world, Brengle—busy as usual in pushing back frontiers, blazing trails, extending borders—was doing week-end meetings at one of his baby corps when, in passing a news stand, a pang smote him in the heart as a headline smote him in the face: "REVOLT LIKELY TO BREAK ARMY RANKS."

The immediate effect upon him was an overwhelming desire to rush to the aid of all the "little people" whom God had called him to serve and who he knew must now be dazed by the blow. In these first moments of The Army's crisis in America, did he hear—piercing through the voices shouting "Rebellion!" "Split!" "American Salvation Army!"—a clarion voice calling him to rally the bewildered forces? On March 10, 1898, two weeks following the announcement of Ballington Booth's resignation, he wrote from Worcester to the Chief of the Staff:

When I wrote you last December that I felt that there was need of The Army's striking deeper root in this country, and that there should be more prayer and heart-searching simplicity and burning holiness in our own ranks, little did I think of the terrific storm that was so soon to smite us, and the way God should call us to heart-humbling and prayer. It is painful beyond measure, but I can only praise the Lord for His faithfulness. I am sure He is dealing with us as gently as His infinite love and wisdom will permit, and only means by this fearful chastening to save us and make us partakers of His holiness, and show the world that The Army is not a man-made institution, but His own handiwork.

If we humble our hearts and seek His face and look only to Him for deliverance, we shall live and yet delight ourselves in fatness. It seems to me that now is the time to strike root, to deal with our own people, to lead them back to the old paths, to make them mighty in God.

With sanctified sagacity he knew that busy soldiers do not rebel. Therefore: "Lead them back to the old paths . . . make them mighty in God!" Press the war against sin! Fight the Devil! Save souls! Divert the attention of officers and soldiers from fighting others; concentrate it on their own spiritual needs and on saving the lost!

This was the method he practiced with remarkable results in his own District. And a month following the "split" he was given a wider field: he was sent to Chicago, a particularly severe storm center at this time, where the Chief Divisional Officer had gone with the dissenters, abandoning hundreds of officers and soldiers to bewilderment. Leaving Mrs. Brengle in temporary charge of the district, he took up his multifarious duties as General Secretary for the North-Western Province comprising Chicago, S. Michigan, Wisconsin, and Indiana.

Here, for three and a half months, he threw himself and his every energy into the breach. Due to necessary frequent absences of his Provincial Commander, much of the responsibility of the Province devolved upon him. During the day he interviewed officers, talked with newspaper men, kept the Province's books, straightened corps accounts, untangled legal difficulties, conducted officers' councils, wrote articles for publication, organized a stir-

ring camp-meeting on the shores of Lake Michigan, and
traveled through his command. His evenings and Sundays
were taken up with public meetings, church services, more
officers' councils, all-nights of prayer, holiness campaigns
—at all points leading enthusiastic attacks on sin and
carnality.

Everywhere, as he traveled about the Province, Brengle
crossed the path of the recalcitrants who, banded loosely
under various ex-officers of The Salvation Army, had at-
tached to their sundry "new movements" such names as
the "American Salvation Army," the "Christian Crusad-
ers," and the "Volunteers of America." And what was his
attitude toward them? Had the unhappy contest soured
his spirit, dulled the edge of his experience? Did he launch
diatribes against the dissenters, denounce them, pray for
their speedy downfall? Not at all. We catch a momentary
glint of tolerance at its sweetest in this brief paragraph
concerning one of the bitterest of the opposition:

> K— is coming here to take charge of the V's. I am praying God
> to thwart his efforts to do us harm, but to bless him if he devotes
> himself to getting souls saved—and I believe God will do it. Glory
> to His Name!

Sometimes reviled, he reviled not again. Soon both
friend and foe knew him to be of metal unalloyed, and
wherever he came the dissension moved off. Conducting
his open-airs, he poached on the preserves of no man,
refusing to engage his troops in sections adjacent to meet-
ing-places of the rival groups, even withdrawing gracefully
when the latter would start operations obviously designed
to embarrass him and take his crowds.

In all his meetings he adhered to the practice of ignoring
talk of discord and rumors of "splits." On spiritual things,
there was laid his emphasis.

To aid him in his campaign for the proper placement of emphasis, he wrote at this time a number of articles for *The War Cry* on the subject of "Soul-Winning." So effective a stimulus did these papers prove that they were later printed in book form. The book, titled "The Soul-Winner's Secret," and containing chapters on Zeal, Prayer, the Soul-Winner's Personal Experience, Keeping the Flock, Saving the Children, Dangers the Soul-Winner Must Avoid, sold widely among Salvationists and early was translated into various languages and printed abroad. A leading staff officer, evaluating it, said: "This book probably did more to turn the minds of our people from self to souls, from the split to the Christ—thus saving them for The Army—than did any other person or agency."

In June, 1896, he received his promotion to the rank of Major, and a month later was appointed to be the General Secretary of the Central Chief Division, under Lieut.-Colonel George French.*

Beginning his work in New York with rapid pace, he continued in the same manner throughout the eleven months of his General Secretaryship. "My head is just about bursting with big plans and propositions for the work here" were the words with which he opened his prodigious labors in New York. In a short time those associated with him discovered that he had an amazing talent for unresting activity.

His experience as District Officer in New England and as General Secretary in Chicago had given him an enlarged appreciation for the movements of a great organization's wheels. If in days prior to entering upon executive responsibility he had thought too little of The Army's machinery

---

* The late Commissioner French.

and too exclusively of its motive power, he now saw them both in better perspective. Reading in his Bible the text, "Thou shalt feed my people Israel, and thou shalt be ruler over my people Israel," he drew his pencil under the words "feed" and "ruler over," as though telling himself that now he understood more clearly the dual relationship of a leader to those under him. His changed attitude is seen, too, in his prayers; according to a diary entry of November 3, 1896, "high spirituality and high efficiency in business" had become twin subjects of his petitions:

I have been thinking and praying today over high spirituality and high efficiency in business. I want to succeed in combining the two. Paul and Wesley and Moses and Daniel and Joseph did it. My heart is full of love for Jesus today. Bless God! He is mine and I am His. Paul says, "I was not a whit behind the very chiefest apostle." I want to be like that. Not selfishly, but for God's glory and the good of man.

Thus he passed his days in a swirl of activity. Faith and works, jump and jubilance, are mingled inseparably in his correspondence covering this period. To Mrs. Brengle, detained at Amenia on account of her aged father's uncertain health, he sent letters that are eloquent of the pressure of detail. And on the envelopes of Mrs. Brengle's letters to him, which he evidently carried about with him for many re-readings, are jotted all sorts of memoranda such as might be made by a man with multifarious duties and a recreant memory.

Despite the way business affairs bulked ever more largely in his day, however, "first things" were still kept to the fore. He had a strict genius for *being* that no talent for *doing* could ever overshadow. Though he had discovered the presence of "Thou shalt rule," he nevertheless remembered that "Thou shalt feed" came first in the brace of commands. With the exception of a few week-ends he spent in Amenia with Mrs. Brengle, his every night was given either to meetings or officers' councils. No amount of necessity for the tightening of bolts and the working of levers could ever make this man forget to look first to the generation of motive power.

Officers of the Division talked among themselves of how understanding he was; many mentioned his office as a place where spiritual wrinkles might be ironed out. Discouraged or disgruntled officers, coming in to resign, went away ashamed of their unspiritual notion. Such a one, coming to Brengle one day in high dudgeon at what he termed the "sauciness and arrogance" of a certain headquarters officer, explained that because of that officer's attitude he simply would not pay a debt owing to headquarters. Brengle listened, then turned up his Bible to Exodus 23:4-5; reading it, they laughed together, read further, prayed, and when the officer went away, he left the money due to headquarters on Brengle's desk, saying, "I saw my enemy's ass going astray, and I have brought him back. Here he is."

On the wall of Brengle's office there hung a text: "Behold an Israelite indeed, in whom there is no guile." His comrades, noting it, would go out to remark how well it fitted the man whose office wall it decorated.

Thus busily, blessedly, guilelessly, did he devote his eleven months in New York to the dual duties of feeding and ruling over his comrades.

When at the end of that period, in response to a "Macedonian call" from the Pacific Coast, he was ordered to close down his desk for what he and his superiors thought was but a brief interlude, he closed once and for all his career as an administrative executive.

Nearer and nearer was he coming to the appointment for which God had, above all else, been fitting him.

Chapter XI

"SPIRITUAL SPECIAL"

Brengle, having just arrived in San Francisco, was seated in the office of Major W. A. McIntyre,* General Secretary for the Pacific Coast Chief Division, under whose direction, in the absence of the Divisional Commander, his campaign on the Coast had been arranged. After conversing for some minutes, McIntyre suddenly turned to Brengle:

"Major, when I asked that you might come to California, I had a double purpose in mind. I wanted you for the Trestle Glen camp-meeting; but I wanted you for myself as well. I've read your writings, sensed your spirit, and I believe you can help me. I've grown a little dry in my own soul. I didn't expect to approach you here in the office; I intended rather to wait and lead the way to the penitent-form at the camp. But I can't wait." After this frank confession of heart hunger, the two men went to their knees.

In such a manner was the way paved for what turned out to be, according to the San Jose *Mercury*, "altogether the most successful meeting of its kind ever held on this Coast." The camp-meeting, opening in a blaze of revival fervor, ran for two weeks, during which more than four

* Commissioner McIntyre, Territorial Commander, Central (U. S. A.) Territory.

hundred came to the penitent-form seeking deeper spiritual experiences.

When the camp had closed, Brengle spent an additional four weeks conducting short campaigns in other parts of the Pacific Coast Chief Division.

It was while on this tour that Brengle became privy to a bit of information that again set ringing within him the bells of a long-lived hope:

He [McIntyre] surprised me this morning by saying that since the Trestle Glen camp-meeting he and [Major] Marshall* and [Staff Captain] Dunham† had bound themselves in a prayer covenant, to pray that God would put me altogether in spiritual work. He is writing [Colonel] Higgins** to suggest strongly that I be used for this work exclusively.

Having learned of this prayer covenant, he allowed his thoughts, for the first time in several months, to dwell on the ambition that had lived with him for years—lived down deep in the cleansed recesses of his heart where in some men dwell selfish aspiration and passion for position. Was his Lord after all going to lead him into evangelistic work? During his stays in Chicago and New York, it had seemed that the Lord was closing that road to him and opening another that tended to leadership of an administrative, as well as spiritual, character.

Only once while in New York as General Secretary had he allowed his stifled wish to speak out. It was at a time when, particularly laden with heavy office routine, he had gone to the Consul, told her he thought The Army was not getting the best out of him as a General Secretary, and

---

* Colonel Stephen Marshall (R), U. S. A.
† The late Lieut.-Colonel David Dunham, U. S. A.
** General Edward J. Higgins (R).

that, if he might be allowed to speak for himself as he would of any other officer, he would suggest that he be put out on the field where he might devote himself entirely to soul-saving work. Since nothing had come of the suggestion, however, he had bowed himself again to the routine, accepting it as God's will for him.

Now, however, significant questions presented themselves: What of these hungry hearts calling him across the country to feed them? What of God so abundantly blessing his labors in this direction? And what of men binding themselves in covenant to pray him into evangelistic work? Were these the finger of God, beckoning him at last to the type of service which, had he chosen for himself, he would have entered upon ten years ago?

A few days later, while engaged in his closing meetings on the Coast, he received a message from New York that brought joy to his heart and a shout to his throat: he was instructed to return to that city at once to farewell from his office as General Secretary for the Central Chief Division—this in order that he might begin immediately upon his new work as the "National Spiritual Special"!

At last—an appointment consonant with his specialized training, his most fervid and secret longings. Back in his Cadet days, three months after joining the Army, he had written: "I sometimes wonder if God means me for a kind of holiness evangelist to The Army. . . ." And through the years that wondering had been ever-recurrent, till now, the appointment in hand, he wondered no more.

National Spiritual Special. Salvation Army terminology for what God calls—a Prophet! In those words he saw, not just another appointment, but destiny.

Reviewing the path along which he had come, Brengle could see clearly the successive steps of God's leading and training. He had given him humble birth, that he might be one with the poor. He had subjected him early to toil, that he might always understand and be able to speak the language of the toiler. He had equipped him with the learning of the schools, that he might be able to enter into the mind and problems of the scholar. He had lifted him high toward ecclesiastic position, that he might be familiar with the ministry of those among whom he was largely to labor. He had brought him low in humility, introduced him to persecution and the hardships of small Army corps experience, that he might be wise regarding the trials of his comrades. He had given him executive position, made him a "ruler over" the flock, that he might have fellowship with staff officers in their multiplied cares. Every step, indeed, along his whole diversified path had contributed to his development, deepened his understanding, widened his knowledge, expanded his sympathies. He had been "all things" and in all places among all men, that he "might by all means save some."

True, the path of his development had been winding, overhung with shadows sometimes, the next step often difficult of discernment. But God had been in it all, and because His man had not faltered nor turned back, He could now lead him out into the open road.

Brengle—God's Prophet!

In his diary that day he made this entry:

"And Samuel grew, and the Lord was with him, and did let none of his words fall to the ground. And all Israel from Dan even to Beersheba knew that Samuel was established to be a prophet of the Lord" (1 Samuel 3:19-20).

What earthly honor or fame can compare with this! What dignity to be—"a prophet of the Lord"!

Chapter XII

CAMPAIGNER

During the three decades immediately following his appointment in 1897 as "Spiritual Special," Brengle's name and message became woven by the flying shuttle of the years in the hearts of people the world over. Tours of America from 1897 to 1904 took him into virtually every state of the Union, while between 1904 and 1910 the pattern was introduced into foreign fabrics, his message being heard in England, France, Sweden, Norway, Denmark, Finland, Holland, Switzerland, Australia, New Zealand, and the Hawaiian Islands. From 1911 on, his evangelistic efforts were concentrated principally upon the American continent.

From the day he entered upon the work to which he felt he was committed by temperament as well as by conviction and appointment, requests that he conduct campaigns, prompted by the reputation he had already gained as a veritable prophet of God, had come faster than he was able to fill them. Forgotten now were those transient ambitions to fit his rounded aptitudes into the square hole of business. On the day he farewelled from New York to enter upon this new phase of his career, he wrote to Mrs. Brengle as follows:

Everybody expresses pleasure at my appointment. They all seem to think it is the one thing needed. I feel it is far better for The Army than that I should be shut up in an office, doing work for which I have no particular taste. Multitudes of our poor officers perish and leave us for want of *spiritual* help and someone to whom they can open their hearts. The Commander and the Divisional Officers are so harassed with a multitude of responsibilities that they cannot meet the need. I believe the Lord will, in a large measure, help me to meet it. I believe, too, there is a spiritual hunger abroad in the land.

With this passion to feed the spiritually hungry burning in his bones, he had not been many months at his work before he discovered how nutritious was his gospel to both rich and poor, learned and illiterate. And, being thus able to meet and bless and help all classes, he soon came to see how large and fertile a field was his, far larger than he had thought possible when first he joined The Army.

At first he was amazed at the love which everywhere came out to meet him. When one of his leaders, returning from an inspection tour over the same ground Brengle had covered, told him, "Everywhere I find your name 'as ointment poured forth,' " Brengle wrote in his diary:

These expressions humble me while they fill me with gratitude to God. O Lord, help me to be worthy!

Humble as he always remained, however, he could not down the consciousness that he had become, in a sense, the arbiter of the destinies of thousands of souls for this world and the next. And the thought gave him mingled solemnity and joy. To take up, night after night, the units that made up his audiences, hold them for a period in the hollow of his hand, and swing them from their drab surroundings of sin and temptation and death toward salvation and victory and life everlasting—ah! this was labor eternally important, infinitely high and holy! Into his journal he poured his passionate desire for greater capacity:

I feel that every moment must be used in doing something for the good of my fellows. Oh, that the Lord would enlarge and enlarge and enlarge my capacity for usefulness, increase my faith, and pour rivers of living water through me. I *know* I want this unselfishly. My heart yearns over the darkness and blindness and ignorance and unbelief and unwillingness and helplessness of the people, and I want to make them see Jesus and get at the secret of His fullness and power and holiness.

An expression that appears often in his letters to Mrs. Brengle is: "Oh, Lily, the joy and glory of helping people!"

All, nevertheless, was not joy and glory. It is well to note here certain phases of sacrifice and denial which would have caused a less consecrated man to have sought another path.

With journeyings more distant and involved than St. Paul's, and with the world more truly his parish than Wesley's, Brengle became The Army's great itinerant. No longer had he a home, in the sense that men usually think of home. Hotels and billets were his abiding places for long periods, while he would often spend one night, two nights, or a week on trains and ships. Only for brief seasons between campaigns did he know the comforting luxury of a home and the sweet ministrations of a loving wife, the sound of childhood prattle and the pattering of little feet about the house, the benediction of an easy chair by his own fireside and the tranquillity of utter relaxation after long hours of nerve-sapping work. By nature domestically inclined, he was condemned by his calling to be a wanderer on the face of the earth.

Further, though great audiences would be his in foreign lands, in his own country he was a prophet not so much without honor as without proper help. While his evangelist contemporaries of other denominations had the aid of soloists, pianists, personal workers, secretaries, advance agents, press representatives and so on, Brengle's entire force through the greater part of his campaigns consisted only of himself and a young officer as soloist and general aide. (Indeed, for two and half years he traveled entirely alone.) Moreover, in many of the cities he visited, advance preparation and advertising of his meetings were totally neglected; while in others, especially prior to the World War, the attitude towards The Army was of so indifferent or even hostile a nature as to render vain any attempt to command for its preachers the ear of the crowd.

To one less certain of his Divine appointment, these oft-repeated experiences of small crowds and lack of co-operation on the part of those who he expected would rally to his aid would soon have chilled his fervor and shot question-marks at his calling. But not so with this man. An instance will mirror for us a common trial and his uncommon triumph over it:

At a certain large city, where The Army had a huge hall and a corps with a glorious past record, Brengle had been led to expect a rousing opening for his campaign. On the first night the hall was lighted, and Brengle went into a back room to pray. The chairs in the hall were waiting to be filled. Into the hall drifted forty-five stragglers. Only forty-five. Several hundred unoccupied chairs stared back their empty defiance. Brengle's eye took in the forty-five,

about twenty of whom were children from poor homes, untidy, unkempt. A few soldiers were present, three or four big boys, a man or two, and the rest were sad or sour-faced women. I had my own songbook and I think there were three others in the congregation. I confess I was sharply tempted to be vexed. What could be done? Was it worth while to try? Would I not better pack up and go home next morning? Should I be expected to spend my strength helping a man with no more spirit and interest than that corps officer?

Then I remembered God. He was interested in these people; Jesus had died for them. They had come in the fierce cold to welcome me. What if the rest of the city was indifferent? Did they not deserve the best I could give them? And as I looked at them they were no longer simply forty-five humble men and homely women and unkempt children. They were forty-five immortal souls, journeying through thronging temptations and trials and sorrows and allurements to the grave, to the Great White Throne, to heaven or to hell. I saw these souls looking out and up at me through dull, hungry, quizzical eyes—looking as though wondering whether I would club them or feed them, give them stones or bread. And my heart was swept with a great pity for them. I rejoiced in spirit, I was eager for spiritual battle. If a thousand of the best people of the city had been present I should not have felt more inspired. Well, we had eight souls that night and at the end of the six days ninety-nine men, women and children had sought the Lord publicly from crowds that grew larger every night. Hallelujah!

In this spirit Brengle often got victory out of what at first had promised nothing but defeat. It should be noted, however, that his victory came not because he was insensitive to his trial; had he been, there were no virtue in his victory. As we have seen, such things as small crowds, due as they often were to human shiftlessness, depressed him. But always he "remembered" in time. The following diary entry for March 15, 1912, when small crowds at unannounced meetings in Minneapolis, Minn., had irked him, reflects the ebb and flow of his spirit:

When the General, or Moody, or Chapman, goes into a city, the whole city takes notice. But when I come, only a handful out of the quarter of a million inhabitants know I am here. Oh, that I might reach the multitudes with the Gospel! I seem so like a man picking up a few handfuls of pebbles here and there along the shore. My heart wants to compass the whole shore!

But I remember that when Paul went into Athens, no one knew it till he began to talk to a few people in the markets; then he attracted attention and they called him a "babbler" and a "setter forth of strange doctrines." Had some great orator or military man come, the city would have been moved. But Paul started influences that have been working with increasing and transforming power in the world for two millenniums. O Lord, Thou canst make my unheralded and unnoticed coming a blessing which shall sweep on through the centuries; I believe it! Thy ways are not as our ways, nor Thy thoughts as ours. Thou wilt gather up our little lives and the trickling streams of our influence into the great river of Thy plans and purposes and they shall go on blessing the universe forever. Help me, O Lord, make me a blessing. Paul was a chained prisoner in Rome, despised and unnoticed by the great, but his influence abides and increases in healing, helping power, and his name lives while the names of the emperors rot and the names of the proud and rich and great of the city have perished. Oh, the irony!

The late Commissioner Charles Sowton remembered the following incident out of his experience when in charge of the Scandinavian work in the United States:

At Providence, R. I., Brengle paid a visit at my invitation to the Scandinavian corps. It was Thursday, the usual half-holiday for the Swedish domestics, so we thought we would try an afternoon meeting as well as an evening one. At night the hall was well-filled, but in the afternoon it rained very heavily and only nine people turned up. I came into the officers' quarters beside the hall and told Brengle that since only nine had come, I would have a short prayer-meeting with them and send them home till the evening when I knew we would have a large crowd. "Certainly not," said Brengle, "these nine have taken the trouble to come long distances at probably great inconvenience on this wet afternoon. I shall go and give them my very best!" He did so, with the result that six out of the nine came to the penitent-form.

Asked on one occasion what was the smallest number he would speak to, Brengle replied, "Well, I usually draw the line at two. But—have you fewer than that?"

While it were foolish to deny that he preferred a large audience to a small one, this man nevertheless knew that the size of the crowd could be no criterion of the results gained. To those who criticized him for wasting energy on the few, he quickly made answer: "I am glad of the privilege of speaking to many or few. Jesus, you know, preached his great sermon on the New Birth to one man, Nicodemus. And His marvelous sermon on the Water of Life was preached to a fallen woman of Samaria. Should I be less alive to the infinite value of an individual soul than was my Lord?"

In the following we may glimpse the personal philosophy which he had developed toward the little, hard corps comprising the majority of his engagements:

> My light was lit to shine where the darkness is, not where all is light and radiance. Again and again I have gone to a corps where the soldiers were all ablaze with light and love, and I have felt: "I am not needed here. I should be instead in the hard and difficult corps where I am really needed." If our people would see this plainly, it would save them many a heartache when they find themselves in a hard place. *That* is the one place where Jesus needs them, and they ought to glory in being chosen to fill it.

Another difficulty that faced him during the greater part of his intense campaigning in America was that, as a rule, his stay at any one corps could be but brief. At most places he spent but three days; at some, less; at few, more than six days. At first the thought that he could do little more than a superficial work in so short a time had tempted him to feel that what he did would not last. In this, however, he had quickly detected what he termed a "failure to believe in the vitality of the Word." In one of his first letters to Mrs. Brengle after beginning his service as a revivalist, he had written:

> One difficulty that I see is that my time is so short. I must reprove, rebuke, exhort, instruct, inspire—all in a day or two—and then run away and trust the Lord to do the rest through such material as the officers may be. I wound people, cut out abscesses,

amputate arms and legs, and take out eyes, but cannot stay with my patients to see how they will heal. However, that is the way Jesus went about, and Wesley, and the General. God can help people without me, and He will. Pray that He will help me to so preach the truth that people cannot escape its power, and that it may so sink into their hearts and lay hold of their understanding, judgment, will and conscience, that it shall have *cumulative force and influence* in their lives.

Later experience proved conclusively that his work did have "cumulative force and influence." Doubling back on his trails of former days he was ever to meet the accumulated forces and influences of his original work. From wherever people had sat under his preaching there would spring up reincarnations of himself and his spirit—Brengle reproductions; in miniature, perhaps, but reproductions nevertheless. So his soul has marched on where his feet have never come. Men preach his sermons and tell his stories in cities he never has visited; and thus his words go on winning victories for his Lord, even in unknown corners and far-away places.

Chapter XIII

PREPARATION FOR PREACHING

ON ONE occasion, when a field officer, harried by a multitude of duties that left him but little time for sermon-making, asked Brengle this question, "If you had but ten minutes to prepare for a meeting, how would you spend it?" he received a reply in two words: "In prayer!"

In that we see definitely indicated the place of heaviest emphasis in his method of sermon preparation. When a young theologian one day asked him, "What preparation do you make for preaching?" Brengle gave answer in which there is meat for the class in homiletics as well as for the biographer:

My lifetime has been a preparation for preaching. But, more particularly, I prepare my sermons for others by preparing my own heart. In this, prayer and Bible study are the chief factors. When I read books other than the Bible, they are read not that parts of them might be included in my address, but to enrich my own thought and to quicken and inspire my faith. Thus I spend a great deal of time preparing myself for preaching. Many make the mistake of giving more time to the preparation of their addresses than to the preparation of their own hearts, affections, emotions, and faith; the result often is beautiful, brilliant words that have the same effect as holding up glittering icicles before a freezing man. To warm others—and is not that your purpose in preaching? —a man must keep the fire burning hot in his own soul.

The large place that the Bible occupied in Brengle's preaching was patent to all who heard him. Scripture quotations were so interwoven through all he said that to lift them out would be to make his addresses almost unintelligible. One hearer sharply etched Brengle when he said of him: "This man is a walking, talking edition of the Bible." Herein, doubtless, lay the tone of authority that pervaded his utterances, causing men when hearing him to think they were listening to a veritable oracle of God. In his prefatory note to Brengle's "Ancient Prophets," General Higgins said in 1929:

Much of the success with which the Commissioner's work as a teacher of practical godliness has met may be ascribed, I am confident, to the place which the Bible occupies in his platform utterances, as well as in the words which from time to time come to us from his pen.

In his public handling of Scriptures, he was graphic, pictorial. While reading Bible stories, his mind would quickly translate the printed narrative into dramatic movement on the screen of his imagination. On many occasions he would break through indifference and frigidity right at the start of a meeting by his ingenuous method of clothing a text with such action. Beginning to read his selected passage in an indeliberate manner, he would break off suddenly to take part in the picture. Thus:

" 'Peter, an apostle of Jesus Christ. . . .' What's that, Peter, how can you make such a claim? Did you not deny Him in His bitterest hour? Did you not turn coward, and curse and swear?' " etc. Forthwith there would be a conversation between Peter and Brengle with the rugged fisherman telling in broken voice of the loving look and the infinite compassion of his Master which gave him reinstatement as an apostle.

Or again: " 'Paul . . . unto the church of the Thessalonians which is in God. . . .' Wait, Paul. Haven't you got your sentence mixed? Don't you mean 'The Church of God which is in Thessalonica'?" etc. And in this utterly naïve exegesis the crowd saw the church and caught at once the significant difference between the readings.

Brengle's notes were scanty—just a few jottings on the back of an envelope or a scrap of paper. While there undoubtedly was an outline, or "skeleton," to his addresses, the latter were so covered with flesh that the lay listener could scarcely tell where or whether the body had any ribs. On many occasions he used no notes at all, and often when he brought them with him to the platform, they would go begging for attention. In his platform delivery, therefore, he was extemporaneous in the finest sense of the word.

Moreover, Brengle's messages were distinctly his own— or, more correctly, God's through him. That is to say, he preached no other man's sermons. What he gave forth was his, as much as direct inspiration from God and a thorough filtration of the best thoughts of great religious thinkers could make it so. His conscience on this point was supersensitive. He felt himself to be a prophet of God, his soul more than a mere repository or distributing agency for what God had given others. It is not that he despised human teachers; indeed, he found much blessing in browsing through the works of the good and great, possessed a considerable library, and was forever buying and reading new books on religious themes. But when it came to preaching, he held that it is the prophet's high privilege to get his messages directly from God Himself. His feeling was that, if preaching means simply a repetition by rote of what others have said, anybody with platform presence and a fair memory might qualify.

Brengle did not have, especially in his later years, a large "barrel" of sermons. His evangelistic campaigns, limited as they were to a few days each, had the tendency to confine him to a rather narrow range of subjects. After entering entirely upon evangelistic work, and finding certain general conditions and needs common to every community and people, he carefully sifted from the mass of subjects from which he had preached an elect few that he found the most pointed, the most applicable, the most productive in souls. These he used again and again. That is not to say that he preached the same sermons verbatim, word for word. Though he clung largely to the same subjects, he was forever introducing new phases of development, fresh illustrations, recent fruits of his more mature thought. Testimony to this is offered by one of his former aides, Major Wesley Bouterse, who, having traveled extensively through America with him and heard the same sermons many times, says: "I never tired of hearing the Commissioner speak. Though I heard them over and over again, his addresses came to me each time new, fresh, virile."

From the standpoint of the people to whom he preached, this constant repetition of a sermon was their gain, since the message must have come to them as perfect as constant practice, pruning, and polishing could make it. Upon Brengle, however, it must be admitted that the advisability of thus confining himself to so circumscribed a range of subjects had a cramping effect. This he realized, and often secretly deplored. While in his writings he found release for many of the things he felt he must express—(his books contain a much wider range of matter than his sermons)—his spoken messages seldom travel out of a restricted area.

In a diary entry for August 2, 1911, he expressed the dangers and drawbacks of evangelism as he saw them. Lamenting that "the life of the evangelist is beset by peculiar hindrances to conscientious preparation and general intellectual growth," he made this further observation:

The evangelist must confine himself to a certain line of subjects, and he must in every new field of labor—which means every week or so—begin all over again. He aims at immediate results. He cannot wait to see the unfolding of character following the preaching of the truth, and gradually loses far vision and becomes spiritually near-sighted. (O Lord, help me. Broaden me out and deepen me in my soul's experience and give me a statesman-like view of truth and of Thy plans for the future of The Army and the Church.)

The evangelist may, by much prayer and meditation and faithfulness, cultivate in himself a sense of responsibility, but the tendency of his work is to destroy or atrophy that sense. He moves about largely care-free. If people do not like him, he does not feel the responsibility of adjusting himself to them, for he soon passes on and hears of them no more. His opportunities for study are limited. He works at high pressure, is surrounded by people, has many public and private engagements, lives in a hotel, or is entertained in some private home, and is away from his library and books of reference. How can he study and make quiet, careful preparation? (O Lord, help me. Keep me fresh and full of compassion and humility and teachableness!)

This, then, is how Brengle—by keeping ever alive to God and refusing to allow his constricted intellectual sphere to hedge in his faith and love and vision—moved through the years a victor over his circumstances. Though his observation of many of his contemporaries had taught him the truth of the words which he underlined in red in a Life of Henry Drummond,* he himself proved the possibility of going on from victory to victory, his soul growing bigger, his heart more fiery, his spirit unflagging, his zeal ever increasing.

And that is the mark and seal of the true evangelist.

---

* A criticism of professional evangelism: "A few years of enthusiasm and blessing, then carelessness, no study, no spiritual fruit, too often a sad collapse."

Another phase of his preparation for his meetings was the Jacob-like wrestlings which preceded almost every victory he won—for other souls and for his own.

I have to fight, it seems, against all hell in these successive campaigns. My soul is almost always in agony for the first day or two. It is the same in every corps. My soul travails in pain and amazement and great heaviness until the great break comes and those who have been struggling with conviction and almost with despair get the victory. Then my heart is full of peace till the following week, when the same fight is on again.

In the above paragraph from one of his letters he bares for us the inward soul-struggle which was his in virtually every place he visited. Principalities, powers, the rulers of darkness, were to him foes as real as though they stood forth clothed in flesh and blood and armor, disputing his every advance, fighting to retain possession of every soul he won. His meetings, especially those which opened his various campaigns, were with him fields of heavy battle, where the fire of the enemy was hot and unceasing. All about him he felt the presence of his unseen antagonists, strongly entrenched, not easily routed.

To Brengle the Devil was no mere figure of speech, no convenient hyperbole for inward tendencies to wrong, no merely nebulous spirit of evil. He was a person, a crafty, subtle, strategic foe, none the less existent for being invisible. Though others might scout the idea of the personality of Satan, he had come to too close grips with his foe to be able to dismiss the Devil simply as another name for evil influence. He said:

I've got to fight my battles with the Devil. I have a pitched battle with him everywhere I go. But it is the battle of other souls I am fighting. When I do get the victory it is a shouting one, and I can go into the fight with my whole soul, conscious that God is with me.

For his meetings, Brengle usually prepared an order of service that had but few items. This insistence upon a simple program he called "clearing the decks for action." There were no long, involved, time-taking preliminaries; such matters as the collection and announcements were the only interpolations allowed which did not bear directly upon the tremendous business in hand: the saving and the sanctifying of the people. An extract from one of his letters describes the order of service which he invariably followed, save for those occasions when he felt led by the Spirit to take some other course:

It is "the old paths." It is not band displays, lectures on The Army, etc., but a rousing heart prayer, a solo from my assistant, the collection, announcements, another solo, a straight sermon, and a red-hot, unhurried prayer meeting and the presence of the Lord revealed in a row of weeping, praying, believing sinners and a lot of rejoicing soldiers.

In all his meetings Brengle was insistent that no more time should be given to introductions of himself than was absolutely essential. He labored under no delusion concerning the stultifying effects of preacher-lionizing.

To minimize the possibility of chairmen committing "the sin of lengthy, flattering introductions," he usually wrote the person under whose direction his meeting was to be held, saying, "Please announce simply, when the time comes, that I will speak. I want to get at the people, and elaborate introductions delay me, as well as dissipate thought and time and energy that should be used to win people for Christ."

In the matter of promoting the desirable atmosphere for his meeting, Brengle's first task was to fuse the aggregation of individuals into unity of thought and expectancy. In this, singing played no inconsiderable part. The meeting was generally opened on the wings of glad, praiseful song, something familiar that everybody knew and would sing. If the person leading the song displayed too rigid a bearing, Brengle would loosen things by taking the book, reading out a verse, and making some homely or whimsical comment on himself or the leader; the audience thereupon would laugh, and be his. Urging the crowd to sing heartily, with abandon, he usually got from them bursts of happy melody, with no thought for consecutive fifths or diminished sevenths or modulated tones—just the spontaneous, beautiful joyousness of religion lifting up a simple tune and making it surge and resound as with angelic harmony.

The second song would be given a more serious aspect; with everyone now united in spirit, it was time to shade the atmosphere with the color of his message. Hence, choosing what he called "one of the grand old hymns, with meat for the hungry, oil for the wounded, balm for the soul"—such as "In Evil Long I Took Delight" or "Rock of Ages" or "Alas, and Did My Savior Bleed"—he "lined it out" slowly and solemnly, his resonant voice calling the words from the frigidity of the printed page and making them vibrant with meaning.

He had advice to give about singing. "Don't sing looking around the room!" he would say; "See this song! Feel it!" On one occasion when someone started the chorus, "All the Way to Calvary," in rapid tempo, he stepped forward, stopped the singing, saying, "Comrades, let's sing this one slowly. Jesus didn't go galloping to Calvary. He struggled beneath the Cross. He fell beneath its weight"—and so vividly did he paint the Passion picture that when the song was begun again, it was heavy with meaning to everyone present. Students at a certain university, too, could tell about the time he put brakes to their singing by saying, "Let's take it more slowly, students. You can't *taste* a song when you sing it so fast. It's like food which you can't get benefit from by bolting it. This song is written to be tasted, digested, assimilated."

Whether his audiences were large or small, he—knowing the advantage of mental communion, the mass receptibility engendered by numbers of people sitting together and concentrating upon one theme—liked to have them compactly arranged. He noted of one occasion: "The congregation was large, but scattered. Their elbows did not touch, and so no contagious interest or enthusiasm was possible."

Thus his concern for advance preparation, a simple order of service, the proper atmosphere, the perfection of setting. To him these items, lightly regarded by some, were contributing factors to the conducting of the most important business in the world. As such, therefore, they had to be as nearly perfect as possible.

Chapter XIV

ON THE PLATFORM

FRAGMENTS of description of Brengle on the platform, supplied by those who have been members of his audience, cast various tints on the palette of any word-painter aspiring to a portrait of "Brengle the Preacher."

Simplicity was one of the dominant colors. Many, themselves skilled in the arts of speech, saw in his simple and unstilted style the utmost development of a man who from his boyhood had courted true eloquence, true force, in expression. As for himself, Brengle spoke primarily to be understood, and, at the time of his beginning on his "Spiritual Special" work, had devoted years to the developing of the art of saying "vast things simply." Remarking on the difficulty of acquiring this unadorned style after having, in his early experience, exercised himself rigidly in the florid oratory of his early contemporaries, he said:

I carefully cultivated the conversational style because I soon saw that it was the most effective in speaking to all classes of people. You may believe that the cultivation took time, for I had all those years of training in oratory, with its flowery and bombastic style, to buck against.

Agencies aiding him in the cultivation of this art were: first, his sanctification, when he became "willing to stammer and stutter"; second, Mrs. Brengle's persistent work at what she called "filing off the remnants of pulpit crust on your tongue"; third, the years of speaking to small crowds of "little people"; and lastly, the necessity in foreign lands of talking through interpreters, which required the use of the shortest, simplest, most easily translated words, and which, as Mrs. Brengle wrote him in her expressive manner, rendered impossible

any shouting and flourishing. A man can't yell, and then stop to be translated, and then go on whooping. It isn't practicable. Nor can he gesticulate wildly, hold his pose while the translator gabbles, and then go on flapping.

In Brengle's conversational delivery, observers saw little of "the pulpit manner": whereases and therefores and firstly-my-brethrens did not figure at all in his discourse. His message always was simple, vital, contemporaneous; in it were no reminiscences of catechisms, no smell of musty tomes or dank ages; and notably absent was that stilted verbiage so lacking in meaning for the man in the street. All he said was truth digested to its simplest possible expression, as fresh and beautiful and sober as Bible language; in words as short as those of "Pilgrim's Progress"; easy to understand; a common-sense saying of the things hungry hearts need to be told. "An admirable mixture of simplicity and sublimity," was a college professor's summing up of Brengle's addresses.

Another trait which impressed those who heard him was his logic. Some compared him with Finney in his manner of preaching Gospel truth as a lawyer pleads his case. Like a lawyer, Brengle had one object in mind: to win his case. Like a lawyer, too, he marshalled every fact of logic, all evidence and all witnesses, to command a favorable decision. Like a lawyer, too, he appealed to irrevocable decisions as found in the Record of the Supremest of

Supreme Courts. Unlike a lawyer, however, he had always a biased jury, a jury that was both jury and prisoner, a jury that he had to persuade to render a verdict against itself!

Another thing that often struck a hearer as he listened to Brengle preach, was his keen and intuitive knowledge of the crypts and crevices of the human soul. Said one: "He can look all through a man's heart—upstairs, downstairs, and in the closets." An editor of a denominational weekly described him as "a psychologist of the heart." A woman, after attending one of his holiness meetings, went home to tell her husband: "I *know* he read my very thoughts. He used up the entire time talking directly to me!"

This knowledge of the human heart, of human nature, was indeed one of the great secrets of his power as a preacher. Because it was his habit to dig through the surface to the subsoil, his forceful, simple, crystal-clear sentences seemed always and in all audiences to strike with irresistible appeal below the surface, down in the substratum of conscience long hid by multiplied unheedings and indifference, and to awaken a sense of guilt when the reason for it had almost been forgotten. Under his preaching, men seemed to read the rolls of their lives with apprehension, and, without his mentioning it, think of judgment, the Great White Throne, their sins and the embarrassment of facing them unforgiven.

And how had he come by this ability? Through a study of two text books: the Bible and his own heart! He said:

The greatest book on psychology is the Bible. He who made the human heart knows it. A girl out in California was "so disgusted" with my preaching—but suddenly one day something hit her and she went home and put her arms around her widowed mother and begged her pardon for her unfilial spirit and came back to the meeting and was sanctified; then she thought I was a wonderful preacher! Psychology doesn't help like the Holy Ghost and an intimate knowledge of God's Word. The Bible fits human needs and hearts like my two hands fit into each other.

What I attack always in my preaching is sin in the heart. That is why men think I know their hearts. The Sermon on the Mount will enable a man to know all hearts, as well as his own, if he studies it, meditates upon it, and prays over it. If he reads Paul's Epistle to the Romans he will discover the deadly nature of sin— not of sins, but of sin. When I came to know my own heart I got the key to every heart.

Yet some may ask, how could a mere knowledge of his own heart, so comparatively guiltless, make him to understand the hearts of others—vile, assailed with sin he had never committed, besieged with temptations he had never encountered? Cannot one imagine persons tormented by difficulties of thought and pangs of passion quite out of his range of experience? And would not his lack of first-hand acquaintance with the more scarlet sins rule him out as an effective prescriber for their cure? His answer:

A doctor does not have to have diseases in order to diagnose and cure them. Neither does a preacher have to have committed all sins to diagnose and prescribe a cure for sin. I never knew by experience murder or immorality, but I knew and know the fountain of corruption in the human heart from which all these sins flow. *Sins* are acts, fruits. *Sin* is the tree. My knowledge of the tree enables me to deal effectively with it; I need not have tasted of the fruits.

Be it said that his sermons were not cut according to the brief pattern of the modern day. He preached long. Yet he was one of the few who could preach at length and yet leave his congregation regretting that the meeting had to close. In 1910 he wrote from Australia:

My difficulty now is in talking too long, but I am trying to reform myself at that point. The people will seldom help me by getting up and leaving. I have been informed here that they will only stay so long; but, bless you, they will stay till 11 o'clock, and we can scarcely get rid of them, and it is hard to stop talking, especially when we have so few meetings.

What is it that held the people? Crowd psychology? Personal magnetism? Neither. Listening to his words, those comprising his audience were wont to find themselves cemented to him by the bond of sympathetic union, the spirit of understanding, a spiritual affinity, a parallelism of heart. And this was so rare and helpful an experience that they often would not leave until driven away. Somehow, said the "little people," this man Brengle seemed to understand stumblers and blunderers; seemed to know how hard it is to live right, to keep one's armor always shining; but seemed, nevertheless, to have for them a prescription wonderfully potent to aid them in coping with congenital and acquired weaknesses and the utter perversity of an evil nature. Despite the fact that he himself never sank low in sin, they felt that a touch of the man "who had been there" ran through all he said; his manner, as they saw it, was the manner of one who had been tempted with all the temptations that beset mankind, and yet had triumphed. Let him talk as long as he wished, therefore; they would stay and hear him out.

His voice, which he himself trained and deepened and developed in his college days, always came in for comment; a *War Cry* representative in 1930 penned this shrewd observation:

His voice has the tonal qualities of a great organ. In the course of his preaching, it runs the gamut of expression. While the dominant chord is soft, mellow, conversational, there are times when it becomes deep-throated and booming like the thunder of God's judgments. . . . Brengle's voice, when one thinks of it, has been remarkably preserved during these many years of preaching in all manner of places; the open-air with its traffic noises and hub-bub, little draughty halls and tents, as well as churches, theatres, etc.

A reporter for the Emporia (Kansas) *Gazette* noted in 1898 that "his voice is of excellent tone, mellow, and exceedingly pleasing to the ear." And, going still further back, Brengle told the following on himself:

One of the first sermons I ever preached was at a colored camp-meeting. It was a missionary sermon, and God blessed me, and they shouted. The next morning a friend of mine came to me and said, "A man down at the north end a mile away heard you last night and said to me, 'Those colored people had a great time last night. I heard that negro preacher away down here, a mile away.' My friend replied, 'That wasn't a negro preacher, that was Brother Brengle!'"

His eyes also held the attention of many. It was felt that they had the look of eyes that were accustomed to pierce into higher heavens and to search deeper depths than those into which the eyes of ordinary men ventured. It was often noted that they had many changing tints and expressions. At times they would be alight with fun, sometimes quizzically humorous. Again they would flash out as though coals of fire were burning behind them. Then, as suddenly, they might take on a grave, sad expression that would color men's minds with sober thoughts.

It was his face as a whole, however, that invariably collected the most comment. Many of the tributes came from children, whose impressions are always expressed with an unconscious naiveté and sincerity seldom found in their more sophisticated elders. One little fellow, returning home after a children's meeting, asked, "Mamma, did you ever see God? Well, I saw a part of God in the face of that man who preached." Another little boy, after Brengle had paid a visit to his home, rushed to meet his father as the latter came from work, to inform him: "Papa, Jesus has been here!"

In a meeting in a certain church a deaf woman sat on the front row of seats. She could hear nothing, only watch Brengle's face. Near the end of the meeting she was discovered softly sobbing, and when the prayer-meeting began she fell at the penitent-form. Her daughter, thinking that perhaps her mother had recovered her hearing, knelt by her side to ask if she had been healed, motioning the question, "Did you hear the sermon?" The deaf woman's answer was: "No, I heard nothing, but I saw Jesus in that man's face."

Yet another factor that had contributed no little to Brengle's power to hold the attention of his audiences was his pictorial manner of preaching. His sermons abounded in similes, so artfully used that the listener was hardly conscious of where the "points" left off, and where the stories illustrating them began.

He never, however, employed the anecdote simply to fill time, or for variety's sake; it had to fit the subject closely, illumine it, and always on its final strands was tied a lesson weightier than the story itself. Moreover, the illustrations he used were not of the heavy, involved, far-fetched variety. Life's smaller common things, odd little happenings, homely objects handled and known by, and events known to, everybody—these he would take up while preaching, turn them over and over in the presence of his audience, and make them illustrate life's grandeurs. His mind seemed to have a spiritual adapter for the things his eyes observed, for almost invariably in familiar objects he saw spiritual lessons.

Instead of expounding at length the "Evidence of Religion," for example, he would tell the story of how Lieut.-Colonel Richard Slater (R) was converted from atheism through the testimony of the little maid who knew she was saved because she now felt impelled to sweep under the doormat—and few of his hearers who sweep at all will ever again come near a doormat without remembering the girl and how she knew she was saved. Or, while preaching, his eye might catch sight of an electric bulb, and, directing attention to it, he would remove it from its common place to give it the high calling of a teacher of heavenly light and power—and forever after, electric light bulbs, in the minds of those who heard him, would burn with an incandescence other than that of physical light. Instead of giving a wordy dissertation on "Neighborly Love," he sometimes called attention to his two hands, saying:

The best neighbors I know anything about are my two hands. They have lived on opposite sides of the street for many, many years, and they have never had a row. If my left hand is hurt, my right hand immediately drops all other business and rushes across the way to comfort it, help it out of its trouble. If one happens to hurt the other, the hurt one doesn't get in a huff and say, "Here, I will not stand for that; you can't treat me that way," and get into a fight. No, no. They are good neighbors. My two hands are members of one another. And Christians should be like that. They are members of Christ's body. They should be as loving, as forbearing, as sympathetic and helpful toward each other as are my two hands.

To bring home to Christians the necessity of maintaining the spiritual glow, there was the simile of furnace care:

The old Founder called a few of us to him on the train one day and said, "Young men, take heed to the fire in your own hearts, for the tendency of fire is to go out." I thought about that, and I said to myself, "Yes, fire will go out unless I do three things: 1. Keep the drafts open. 2. Keep the ashes and clinkers shaken out. 3. Put on more fuel." Then I applied it to my own soul. I am not to run around and kindle my fire at the altar of someone else. I have a fire of my own. I am to keep the drafts open—keep testifying, keep the windows open toward heaven. I am to keep the ashes out—I cannot depend upon past experiences; I must seek God afresh. Then I must add fuel—pile on new truth, search the Scriptures, feed my soul. The blasts of hell will blow out the flame if I don't guard the fire in my own heart!

And there are other examples of his allegorizing which his hearers never forgot, and never remembered without recalling also the lesson to which they gave light and life; as, to mention a few: the black bondslave who became a voluntary "love-slave" to the man who had purchased him and then freed him; the stretcherbearer who "got even" with an insulting, wounded enemy by bearing him tenderly away to the doctor's care; the Christian Armenian nurse who, called to attend a desperately ill Turkish soldier whom she recognized as the slayer of her brother, fought a battle with the spirit of revenge in her which said "Just neglect him!", but, remembering her Lord's command concerning the love for and treatment of one's enemies, nursed him back to life and by her example made him plead: "I never knew there was a religion in the world like that. Tell me about it, for I want it, too."

Such stories as these are stories with tears and short catches of the voice in them, touching the heart in tender places. To the same category belongs, too, his story of the little imbecile girl—the only feeble-minded member of a family of strong, healthy girls—who, noticing the other girls gathering flowers for their father's birthday, went out under the constraint of a heart that loved none the less for a faulty mind to guide it correctly, and, gathering a "bouquet" of sticks and straws, presented them to father, noticing that he choked a little as he put her poor little offering in the chief place on the mantelpiece, while assigning the gorgeous floral offerings of the others to less conspicuous positions in the room.

Another attractive phase of Brengle's graphic manner of preaching was the element of stage-playing which he often introduced to animate his word pictures, causing men to say that "he is an unconscious actor; often his sermons become a dramatic piece of consummate art." For example, in giving his version of how Paul, in prison and chained to a Roman guard, reasoned with and won the guard to Christ, he would act it all out—with himself in the rôle of Paul and anyone who happened to be on the platform with him as the Roman soldier. And in the "act," the audience usually found it easy to forget Brengle and his conscripted fellow-actor, while seeing instead the zealous "little hook-nosed Jew" and his burly guard. A college president who, presiding at one of Brengle's lectures at his school, unexpectedly found himself drafted into the latter's *dramatis personæ*, afterward referred to it as "the most impressive piece of Gospel dramatization I ever witnessed."

Three types of sinning particularly stirred him to sternness: immorality, presumptuous refusals of God's mercy, and pharisaism. Against these he trained his guns with an accuracy that was neither temporizing nor equivocal, and hardened indeed was the wayfarer walking these paths who could stand unmoved before the onslaught of truth he hurled. Audiences listening to him dealing with such issues long remember the extreme conviction, earnestness and gravity which they saw stream from his eyes like a torrent. Describing his own feelings and inner reactions after having spoken on one occasion at a school in Kalamazoo, Michigan, where he had been apprised of the prevalence among the students of gross immorality, for which, indeed, a number of the students were in jail, and where his address had resulted in wholesale confession and forsaking of sin, Brengle said: "I felt much as I suppose the angel of the Apocalypse felt in declaring the terrors of the Lord."

A phase of his preaching that was specially noted, however, was that he relegated neither reward nor punishment exclusively to the hereafter. He had a way of seeming to move the future into the present. When he preached, both bliss and brimstone moved, as it were, out of the obscure tomorrow and stood enchantingly desirable or revoltingly terrible in the living today. Under his preaching, men were led to think not so much of melting and cosmic cataclysms as of present sins and immediate shame; not so much of golden streets and seraphic music as of the gold of grace and the joybells of holiness. For those who heard him, today became both the day of salvation and of damnation. To the sinner, his preaching was indeed a savor of life unto life, or of death unto death—and that present and immediate.

Because of this feature, his preaching was "modern" in the best sense of the word. He was never heard to prate unduly about the "old-time religion," as though the choicest spirituality was confined to a day long past. Men gathered that his religion was timeless as God is timeless; that his Christ was not a "period" Christ. Salvation from sin, heaven, hell, righteousness, deviltry—these he knew to be modern, up-to-date. Therefore Christ, their curse or cure, is modern. His Lord, though the Ancient of Days, is, nevertheless, "the same . . . today and forever" as well as "yesterday." In a word, his Christ has scope.

Chapter XV

PENITENT-FORM

THE penitent-form was the immediate goal, the focal spot, toward which Brengle's every point in his meeting technique turned.

Besides being the place to which he drew tens of thousands during the active years of his service, it was also within the penitent-form's sacred precincts that he learned much that he knew of the peculiar impulses and passions of the human heart. Here, kneeling beside penitents in the throes of conviction and confession, he met and battled with the stark forces that move men to all manner of deeds of evil. Here, among the tangled and baffling cross-weaves of the heart, he made contact with the spitework of human tongues, the inordinate animus of those eager not for purity but position, the unforgiving hatreds showing dull and hard in the eyes of persons wronged and waiting for a day of revenge, the shifty look of the guilty, the frightened stare of those with sins threatening to find them out.

If one would take the full measure of Brengle's genius and heart as a soul-winner, he must look here, watch him at close grips with these things which, being found among all the kindred of Cain and Jezebel, David and Bathsheba, Ananias and Sapphira, Judas and Achan, are the very stuff of unregenerate life. Brengle on the platform was mighty. But Brengle at the penitent-form was mightier.

See him:

The dramatic hour is on. Souls are bared. The great transaction between man and his God is under way. Here the streams of life are changing their courses. Being altered are characters, destinies. Being settled, once and for all, are old scores between man and God, and man and man. The penitent-form is shrouded in an atmosphere now like that of a surgeon's operating room, now like that of the drawing-room of father's house when the prodigal returned. Condemnation, contrition, confession, mingle their voices with supplication, gladness, shouts of victory. "Hallelujah!" is a word heard frequently as the penitents "come through."

Down at the penitent-form, having left the singing and additional exhorting to others, Brengle is busy at work directing his seekers into the Kingdom. One by one he deals with them. Salvation is not made easy. The blessing sought by some comes at a higher price than they had expected. He makes it plain that before God can impart forgiveness for sin, reparation, restitution, redress of wrongs must be made where possible, or at least sincerely determined upon and pledged. Neither is holiness to be found in a desultory fashion; one must put away all un-Christlike things, forgive one's enemies, consecrate one's self wholly to God, claim in steadfast faith His promises.

With grace and tact, Brengle wields the weapons with which the Spirit provides him, and in such a manner that no bruised reed is broken, no smoking flax quenched. He has no set formula. His dealing with the penitents is individual in the highest degree. Each seeker must be considered as having a particular and peculiar malady with its own cause and complications. Always his first endeavor is to lead the penitent himself to state clearly his trouble; he has found that many come forward with but vague ideas, scarcely knowing themselves what they want and having not the slightest idea how to find it. To have the seeker himself explain his need clarifies the issue, brings it out of the fog to where it can be dealt with in the broad light of day.

In all his work here, it is marked how constantly he uses his Bible. Of the sum total of words spoken to the penitents, by far the majority are Scripture quotations or readings. Regardless of the nature of the case before him, Brengle in an instant can turn to a host of promises that exactly fit the need. These he makes the seeker himself read and repeat again and again, until the struts and braces of the Word enter his soul and lift him to his feet with a consciousness of new strength, new stability, new life. Then there are the Bible stories; and in a flash Brengle can have before the penitent Magdalene or murderer, Pharisee or fanatic, a compelling narrative of how the Lord saved or blessed his type and kind of centuries ago.

Mark, too, how patient he is! As he moves about among the seekers, it is not with the air of one in a hurry to get over with it. He takes his time, making as certain as he can that all understand fully what they are doing, why they are here, and what they may expect to receive. If there is a particularly difficult case, one who requires much time to fight out his battle, Brengle will be the last one to leave his side. If the seeker be an unusually hopeless example, it is often he alone who has faith to envision a future crown of glory for one with feet so persistently clay and a heart so obstinately black.

Yet he seriously objects to over-dealing. He knows that too much dependence must not be placed on human exhortation. He knows, as well as does the most astute sales manager, that overdoing "high pressure" selling methods too often reacts unfavorably upon the customer. Especially is he anxious that seekers at the penitent-form be not bombarded with too much human advice. Setting down for a comrade-officer the essential points of effective dealing, he once wrote:

Permit me to suggest that, when people have reached the penitent-form, they be allowed to kneel in silence before the Lord for a time without having two or three people come to question them and pour advice into their ears. Give them an opportunity to listen to God's voice, and then let some wise soul go to them and say, "Is there anything I can do to help you, or do you prefer to pray in quiet yourself?" We must not hurry people into the Kingdom at the penitent-form. Give God a chance to deal with them. A friend of mine had an incubator, and one day the little chicks were hatching. He watched them. Some picked their way through the shells quickly, and began to feed. Others had a great struggle. He took pity on some of these and helped them. But, he said, all those that he helped died. They needed the struggle to be born in order to gain strength to live. If we help souls too much at the penitent-form, we may do them more harm than good. Give God a chance!

Note how wise he is in making his altar call. Directly his message is delivered, he invariably gives the first appeal himself. The appeal is specific, but it is not confined to any one class of seeker. Listen:

There is one here whom I want to see lead the way. It is that man, that woman, that boy or that girl, *to whom God has spoken*. I spoke to your outward ear, but He whispered to your inward ear. You are the one that should come first. Let everyone pray and believe while that first one to whom God has spoken comes.

There is a pause, while the atmosphere is heavy with consciences in conflict with decision. Then one comes, followed by another, and by others. In his repeated invitations there are no tricks, no artifices; he has no merely clever methods of entrapping men into this greatest of all decisions. Nevertheless, especially when there is little response to the call, he is an opportunist, quick to seize upon any strategy that will throw his prospective "prisoners" off their guard, ready to resort to unexpected tactics if these will help to push the convicted across the line of decision. On occasion, having spotted one who he feels is moved but unyielding, he will walk slowly down the aisle during the prayer-meeting, looking in another direction until, coming opposite his prey, he will turn suddenly, put his hand kindly on the man's shoulder, saying: "You're not saved, brother? Come with me to Jesus!"—and almost invariably the man comes. Again, noticing that a person who, obviously under conviction, night after night leaves the hall before the invitation has been given, Brengle states at the beginning of a meeting: "We will have the penitent-form first tonight"—and gets his man. Occasionally, too, he does away altogether with the sermon; as, for example, he did on the following occasion:

My singer had no sooner begun his solo than a backslider of seventeen years leapt to his feet and came to the penitent-form. I said: "Since the Holy Ghost seems to have taken charge of the meeting, there will be no preaching tonight. Anyone else who wishes to come, let him come." And how they came! That morning we had a penitent-form full—and seventy or eighty souls for the day.

He proves, moreover, that the altar of God is no stationary object; if people won't come to the penitent-form, then take the penitent-form to the people! As proof of the efficacy of such a move, he could tell the following:

Unable to get any one to the penitent-form in one meeting, I finally got a man on his knees at the door just as he was going out. So I suggested that we move the penitent-form to the other end of the hall, which was done, the soldiers flocking down en masse. When that man got through, we turned our attention to a backslider in the rear, and soon the new convert and the rest of us were down around him—and he got through. Then a young lad near the door gave in and got beautifully saved. Finally there was only one un-saved person left in the hall—the backslidden wife of the Sergeant-Major. We all turned our attention to her and soon she was on her knees in the middle of the hall, where she got saved. So we ended with every sinner in the hall converted. It was a blessed time. It is most interesting to turn the whole hall into a penitent-form!

And look at his converts. They were made up of all the multiplied types, colors, ages, and conditions comprising the kaleidoscopic pattern of humanity. There were con-versions of the most miraculous character; conversions that cost and cost mightily; conversions that meant resti-tution: murderers giving themselves up, deserters from government services going back to irons, law-breakers and fugitives from justice voluntarily going to prison, adulter-ers confessing and forsaking evil, embezzlers making good their defalcations.

In the host of those who found redemption at his peni-tent-forms were mayors and aldermen, as well as brick-layers and draymen; professors and scholars, as well as children and illiterate; ladies of society, as well as women of the streets; persons who could trace noble ancestry, as well as persons who had no ancestry they cared to trace. Often the conversion of a town's outstanding incorrigible caused city-wide notice, resulting in crowded halls and many penitents, drawn from the high ranks of the un-reachables as well as the low rabble of the untouchables—all interested in a God who could work miracles in needy souls.

Chapter XVI

SANCTIFIED SANITY

DEPTH without breadth is narrow; breadth without depth is shallow." Men said of Brengle that he was deep. But they also said that he was broad. His preaching was not the sounding of a single note, a tuneless twanging of one string of the Gospel instrument; it was the striking of a complete chord, full and vibrant.

Much of the blinding glare that shone from his early preaching became, with the passing years, subdued and suffused into softer tints and more beauteous patterns. The picture he painted of the Spirit-filled man's tolerance of the theological tenets of others may well be taken as a self-portrait:

He is tolerant of those who differ from him in opinion, in doctrine. He is firm in his own convictions, and ready at all times with meekness and fear to explain and defend the doctrines which he holds and is convinced are according to God's Word. But he does not condemn and consign to damnation all those who differ from him. He is glad to believe that men are often better than their creed, and may be saved in spite of it; that, like mountains whose bases are bathed with sunshine and clothed with fruitful fields and vineyards, while their tops are covered with dark clouds, so men's hearts are often fruitful in the graces of charity, while their heads are yet darkened by doctrinal error.

To describe the contentious sectary, dead certain he is right and safe, and equally certain his fellow believers of another denomination are wrong and lost he had a saying:

"Some folks are not only dogmatic. They are *bull-dog-matic*!"

For dealing with those whose faith had been cut adrift from what he considered foundation principles, he prayed for understanding. It is not that his zeal had grown cooler; rather was it that his charity had grown warmer. Into his diary, on November 27, 1926, he whispered this meditation:

> I must never become embittered against men. I must pity the man whose faith has been staggered by modern study and discovery, the evolutionist who has lost his Heavenly Father, who harks back to his cave ancestors instead of remembering his divine origin and destiny. Poor soul, he has lost so much and he will have such a hard and stony way to retrace. Help me, O Lord, to understand him, pity and not condemn him, and, so far as I can, help him.

Doctrinal dissentions and ritualistic controversies occupied none of Brengle's time or thought. He had no war to wage upon any believer concerning the abracadabra of his particular faith. Orders, rites, ceremonies, precedences —these he had always left severely alone. Not because he doubted their worth or place, but because to him they were trivial, marginal, irrelevant. He knew the place where lay the need for fight. And at the battle center he ever concentrated all his powers.

In his own message, only those doctrines which could be expressed in and through human experience were allowed a hearing. He was vitally interested only in those "certainties in religion that are not settled by debate, but by tasting and seeing that the Lord is good." For he knew that doctrine written in experience is the only doctrine that cannot be argued against. Observe the recurrence of the word "know" in this passage:

The truth can be known and not simply guessed at. . . . Some doctrines can be verified in soul-satisfying experiences. When a man, broken-hearted on account of his sin, looks to Jesus, seeking forgiveness, and the burden rolls away, he *knows* it. When he passes from the death of sin into the life of holiness, he *knows* it. When the Holy Spirit reveals Christ within him, he *knows* it. When the Bible suddenly flames with light, revealing all the hidden things of his secret life, the deep needs of his soul and all God's ample provisions of grace, he *knows* it. When Jesus, whom he despised, suddenly becomes to him altogether lovely, and the will of God, which was to him a galling yoke, now becomes his delight, he *knows* it.

It is, therefore, this "know so" doctrine that fell from his lips into the hearts of people the world over, bringing them joy, comfort, salvation, the ecstacies of grace. "Simple folk," he said, "want religion with surety. They are not interested in theological hair-splittings, speculations, theories, ologies, isms." Always, we may notice parenthetically, he suited his message to "simple folk," "little people."

In his riper years he came to depend less and less upon set statements of theology, believing that every thoughtful Christian, actually if not consciously, became his own theologian. In support of this, he wrote:

There is a sense in which every thoughtful, studious, prayerful Christian . . . works out, under the leading of the Holy Ghost, his own theology, and discovers what he believes to be the true doctrines of the Bible. He may accept the teachings or doctrines of his parents and religious leaders, and hold them intellectually, but his theology is really limited to those articles of faith which vitalize his life, guide and inspire his conduct, mold his spirit, comfort and guard his heart, purify his nature, and kindle his hope for the future.

Thus we see that the broad-of-soul Brengle, having escaped the bondage of the thousand and one little cords of creed and doctrine that so hamper many another man of

God, advocated *experience* as the proving-ground for the worth of all articles of faith. "As I grow older," he said, "my faith becomes more and more simple. What a mistake to so crowd one's faith with furniture that there's hardly room for the folks!"

Because he early learned of the breadth of God's love, he always hesitated before granting that any living man or woman had passed beyond the pale of God's mercy. Back in the days at Danbury Corps there had been an old sinner, eyes glazed by long iniquity, who sat on the front seat in every meeting. Brengle, having preached to and at him for months without being able to move him, finally decided that this man had sinned away his day of Grace. But—

Years later I returned to Danbury, and whom should I find but this very man, in uniform, and sitting on the platform with the other soldiers! I wanted to go to the penitent-form for my lack of faith. I have learned from that and other lessons not to judge too quickly of a man's "sin against the Holy Ghost"—have learned, too, that the "love of God is broader than the measure of man's mind, and the heart of the Eternal is most wonderfully kind!" *Since that day I have never seen a man who, I have decided, was beyond hope.* "While life lasts, the love of God is reaching out."

* * *

In the early decades of the Twentieth Century, irrational emotionalism took heavy toll of the holiness movement.

To the popular mind, especially in America, a "holiness preacher" came to mean a fanatical bawler; "Pentecostalism" was associated with rolling on the floor to the tune of a sensuous chant and disorderly hullabaloo; the "Baptism of the Holy Ghost" was synonymous with wild eyes and a wilder tongue, the unintelligible gibberings of which purported to be a gift from heaven in token of the Spirit's incoming. Indeed, so confused had holiness become with its unscriptural variants that the Church as a whole, as well as the world, began to shy away from any mention of the doctrine.

Brengle, to his deep sorrow, witnessed the words "holiness" and "Pentecost" being thus degraded from their proper and revered definitions in the ecclesiastical vocabulary and becoming terms used by many to denote religion on the loose. And, because the teaching concerning the baptism of the Holy Spirit was forsaken largely in favor of illicit traffic in fanatical counterfeits of the doctrine, he saw the Church at large quietly close its doors to the Upper Room and relegate to the background the teaching of the higher life, with the result that many of the hungry-hearted became entangled either with irresponsible groups where the sensations were accented and the perceptions excised, or with cults where reason was exalted and emotion frowned upon.

It was also evident that the orthodox religious press had come to regard the doctrine and practice of holiness, as one wrote it, as "a smear of emotionalism," and its prerequisite as "the acquiring of the shibboleth of an 'unknown tongue' before one may become a candidate for sainthood—or that brand of it that is held up by 'holiness' and 'Pentecost' sects."

Plainly, such words as "holiness" and "Pentecost" were in dire need of being redeemed. That Brengle did wherever he went. It is not too much to say that one of his greatest contributions to the Church universal were his representation of a religion that is high and deep coupled with a mind that is sober and sane.

As Brengle became more widely known among church-going people, this reputation for sane sanctity and sanctified sanity spread, so that when the name Brengle was mentioned in church circles, those who knew him told the others that here was a man who preached and lived holiness and yet had maintained his spiritual balance, had not slipped his eccentric, had not allowed his lens to get out of focus. It was readily seen that he had attained that ideal combination of the exemplar Christian: glowing emotion and cool perception.

The cause of the damage done to the holiness doctrine was well understood by Brengle. He knew, as do only those who know human nature, the destructive power of unleashed emotion. He knew emotion to be a fire, warming and useful when correctly applied, but destructive and demoralizing when out of control. For this he had a very apt saying: "Formalism will leave your house cold and freezing; fanaticism will burn your house down." To express the necessity of the counterpoise of mind with heart, he said: "Let your love and your light keep pace. Keep them in equal proportion. Otherwise your love may lead you into fanaticism, or your light may lead you into cynicism."

It was not Brengle's forte to excite a fever of enthusiasm which, when the pulse falls, leaves the subject wan and dejected. His rather was the capacity to incite to earnest heart-scrutiny, and to create a hunger for God which, when persisted in, leads always to deep penitence and soul satisfaction. In his meetings he gave no encouragement to hysterical manifestations. He realized that to permit unrestrained emotionalism was to sail among rocks and through treacherous waters.

In dealing, however, with those whose light had not kept pace with their love, and who had toppled over into fanaticism, it was not in him to slash and slay and denounce. He realized with Fénelon that "all the maddest passions that transport mankind were only the true love gone astray from what should be its center." Looking closely, he recognized in much of the fanaticism abroad the unguided error of "little people" who, searching for depths, had got into shallows where, feeling the breakers, they had mistaken them for the surge of the deep sea tide. He seemed to hear, even in their unintelligible babblings, and see, even in their writhings and rollings, the pitiful protests and plaintive calls of his "little people" for something more real than ritual, something more satisfying than ceremony. And his heart went out to them.

Writing to advise a Divisional Commander about dealing with a young woman officer who had drifted into radicalism and was about to be dismissed, Brengle said:

I wouldn't dismiss S——. I'd labor with her. The poor thing was probably starved. She needs help. She is a hungry soul, and nobody has fed her with "food convenient" for her, and she has stumbled into this error and hungrily eaten what isn't good for her. There are two kinds of people who fall into a snare like the Tongues. Good people who are so afraid that they will miss what God has for them that they will take up with every new thing without trying the spirits, and bad people who like to be conspicuous and are led captive by the Devil at his will.

Neither was he unreasonable nor impatient with those who were seeking to walk in the light they had. He would not too quickly shoot up the standard of perfection before a soul just emerging from the bogs of sin. He had travelled far since the days in Taunton and Danbury, where his enthusiasm for holiness prompted him to strictness not consonant with the capacity of his soldiers. When on one occasion he overheard a zealous comrade heckling another with: "Take it or leave it, brother, it is holiness or hell!", Brengle interrupted the exhortation to say, "Not so. No justified soul will be in hell. But the justified man must walk in the light he has, or he will backslide. And walking in the light will eventually lead him to take the step that will give him a clean heart as well as a justified soul."

Nor would he push a man too rapidly. Speaking to officers in council on the leading of uninstructed souls into the higher life, he said: "You must warm a man gradually! Get down to his temperature. If you try to bring a frozen man too quickly to the fire, you may ruin him, or cripple him for life."

Brengle's own prayer, offered especially when persons were slow to respond to the call to higher things and when he was tempted to deliver an ultimatum, was: "Lord, help me not to be impatient with Thy sheep! They may be diseased and wilful and wayward, but help me to remember they are not wolves. Help me to feed, not club, Thy sheep!"

Moreover, he lived under no delusion that holiness would ever become popular, in the sense that it will be generally sought after, nor did he encourage those who preached it so to believe. The unpopularity of holiness, he held, is the unpopularity of Jesus:

Dear brother, do not think you can make holiness popular. It cannot be done. There is no such thing as holiness separate from "Christ in you," and it is an impossibility to make Christ Jesus popular in this world. To sinners and carnal professors, the real Christ Jesus has always been, and always will be, "as a root out of a dry ground, despised and rejected of men." "Christ in you" is the "same yesterday, today and forever"—hated, reviled, persecuted, crucified.

Such, then, was Brengle—and his well-rounded, well-balanced, sanctified sanity. Such were the deep-running undercurrents of his religion, from which men heard, not the spurious splashings of surface emotion, but the surging tides of ebbless purity. Does one wonder that thousands of the serious-minded, the world over, hungrily sought in him a map of the way of holiness and a model of its practice? Of those who have studied the model and followed the map, we have no better example than J. L. Brasher, D.D.* Dr. Brasher speaks for himself:

In April, 1900, while pastor of the Simpson Methodist Episcopal Church in Birmingham, Ala., I received a pressing invitation from the officer-in-charge of the local corps of The Salvation Army to attend a three-day revival campaign to be conducted by Colonel S. L. Brengle. I read the circular detailing the meetings, and was impressed by the Colonel's scholarship. I went to the first meeting. His face charmed me, his heart caught me, but his mention of "holiness" aroused all my combativeness. I had been an opponent of the doctrine of the Second Work of Grace, and considered it illogical, contrary to psychology, etc. But I could not help being interested by his non-ranting, simple, straight-forward handling of the subject. And not only interested, but shall I say, concerned. I invited him to my study for a conference. He came the next morning. I opened my heart to him as I never before had done to any living being. He made very little comment, simply saying, "I think sanctification will fix you." That was hard to take.

But I was at the afternoon meeting. At the conclusion of his sermon, he asked all who wanted a clean heart to stand. I stood, the only one. Then he asked all who wanted to be converted to stand. A poor old drunken toper and a street-walker stood. Then he invited us to the penitent-form. I led the procession, followed by the bum and the wanton woman, and, when presently I looked around, one was on either side of me. It was a bitter pill for the pastor of a large church, graduate of a celebrated school of theology, with some excellent prospects for the ministry, to be thus humiliated. But I determined to make the most of it, and charitably—I thought humbly— including my mates at the penitent-form, I began to pray: "O Lord, we—," when the Colonel broke in with: "Not we, brother, pray for yourself!" I prayed for myself, made the consecration after Brengle had dealt gently but definitely with me—the while being careful, I thought, to avoid a debative approach—and at the next meeting testified modestly to the Blessing. He said, "I am glad for that

* For many years the beloved president of John Fletcher College, University Park, Iowa.

testimony, brother. Don't be afraid of terms, don't be afraid of the Second Blessing."

Thus it was through his instrumentality that I entered into the Canaan of Perfect Love. His skill and wisdom and approach made possible results that no logic or arguments could have produced, though his addresses were logic itself. I regard him with almost worshipful love. I owe more to him than to any man alive. I have often thought that God sent him to Birmingham purposely to bless me.

Chapter XVII

CHILDREN'S MEETINGS

His contemporaries said of him: "Brengle has a way with the children"—sometimes in a tone indicating that they regarded this a scarce quality in preachers of the sober Gospel. One man seemed to think it "surprising the way the young people are attracted to him"—as though Christlike holiness and vibrant youthfulness were states incompatible in the very nature of things.

But to those knowing well both the man and his Master, this response to Brengle on the part of youth is a condition at once natural and revealing as to his character. Jesus appealed to the young, and, since life always answers to Life, what was more natural than that He should? Therefore, does not the fact that Brengle attracted, was interested in, and won the children, clearly indicate that his brand of saintliness—judged in the ingenuously keen mind of the child—was patterned closely after that of his Lord? Since the young are generally shy of starched saintliness, meticulous virtue, mawkish piety; since they are often afraid of, or amused by, a man in clerical garb, of whatever pattern; and since grey hair and whiskers are usually to them the badges of old-fogeyism, may it not be said that Brengle's triumph over youth is the triumph of the Christ wherever, and by whomever, He is properly expressed?

In Brengle the young saw unaffected goodness. But

they saw more: they saw goodness that was friendly, winsome, compelling, tender—above all, approachable. They felt natural in his presence. More, they sensed that his religion was natural, that it fitted life.

He believed in "a good time." To a young girl who had been frightened away from religion by a gloomy representation of it, he wrote one day:

Major S—told me something funny yesterday. She said that when she was about seventeen she concluded that she ought now to act like a woman, and so she stopped laughing, and felt it wrong to be glad and almost a sin to be happy. I wonder if that is common with girls of that age? You must not fall into such a mistake. God makes birds to sing and puppies to play, brooks to babble and winds to whistle, and He means young people to be happy and glad. Of course, He wants them to be thoughtful and good. But He would have them laugh and rejoice and be glad all their days, only their gladness must be in harmony with goodness and their happiness consistent with holiness. Boys and girls and young men and young women who are Christians ought to be the very happiest people in the world, and ought to let their lives scatter sunshine and gladness to everybody about them. . . . When God gave me a clean heart I wept for joy and laughed down to the soles of my feet. "Be glad in the Lord, ye righteous"—so David sings. "Rejoice evermore," says Paul. And Nehemiah assures us that "The joy of the Lord is your strength."

Here, obviously, was no soured and senile old man, impatient and irritable with children; austere and forbidding, with a bundle of "Thou shalt nots!" in each hand. He was as youthful as they, as bubbling over with merriment, as happy, as joyous. Here, indeed, was a man like that other Man who said: "I am come that they might have life, and that they might have it more abundantly"—and was not speaking only of life beyond the stars—and who spoke of giving His joy that their joy might be full. Is it any wonder that Brengle's spirit brought response from youth, insurgent against long-faced religion, unconcerned with promises and threats of worlds to come, since they have this world and its beauties, and death seems too remote to cause them worry? He recommended religion to them, not as preparation to die, but as preparation to live; not as grave insurance, but as life assurance.

Brengle had ever realized that the best hope for The Army's being made pure and strong lies in the young people. Always, therefore, whether speaking or praying, he saw them before him. Remembering the needs of his own lonely, questioning, aspiring youth, he thought of theirs. When conducting a campaign lasting several days, he tried to arrange at least one special meeting for young people. In many of these meetings he had met with remarkable results, hearing from his youthful converts through many years thereafter.

There is a sense in which all his meetings were children's meetings. Knowing with the astuteness of an expert psychologist that all, old and young, are but children at heart, he filled his addresses (as we have seen) with stories vitally interesting to all, and especially to those who liked to learn by picture rather than by precept. Sorting over his sermons and writings, one seldom comes across a word that children of primary school age could not understand. His talks abounded in stories about children; he used their hopes and fears, fancies and petulance, dependence and affection, to carry many a point. Thus, by use in illustration and by direct address, the children in every meeting were given attention. His feeling about them was:

I am increasingly convinced that in every meeting where there are children present something should be said that is suitable to them, and the invitation to come to Jesus should include them. . . . When they do come, they should be dealt with most thoroughly, their sins searched out and repentance required. Their fears must be tenderly removed by showing them the fulness of God's love and the certainty of salvation when they give up sin. Their thought should be turned to Jesus and their faith fixed on Him and grounded in His Word.

In the place in his heart reserved for precious memories, Brengle carried many stories of children converted in his meetings, many of whom have since grown to manhood and womanhood, having stood true to the decisions then made. One he particularly liked to tell is this:

I had a children's meeting one Saturday afternoon in Wilkes-Barre, Pa. Twenty-three little ones were at the penitent-form. At one end there was a little boy. I knelt beside him and said, "Darling, what do you want?" He said, "I want to get saved from my sins." "What are your sins?" I asked. He replied, "I quarrel with my little sister." I said, "Suppose your little sister should get sick and die, and suppose you looked into her cold dead face and you remembered how you had quarreled with her. Wouldn't you be sorry?" He said, "I would." We prayed together, and he got saved. Finally I came to the other end of the penitent-form and saw there a sweet little girl. "Darling, what do you want?" "I want to get saved from my sins. I quarrel with my brother." She was at one end, he at the other! I applied the same questioning to her, and she burst into tears, we prayed, and she trusted. When they got up, they ran and begged each other's forgiveness and went home and told their mother. Both are now officers. In 1928 when I was lying in the hospital, a young officer was chosen to give me his blood in a transfusion. When I looked across the table to see who it was, it was that little boy.

Another of his favorite stories had to do with "Bolshevik," the young leader of a boy's gang in Chicago, who, standing near an open-air ring formed by soldiers of one of the corps, was captured by Brengle, taken arm-in-arm with him to the hall, and was converted; in time he got his friends to take the same step, and two years later he and all his gang were formed into the junior band of that corps.

With the passing years his interest in children and their

salvation grew even more intense. He got out a booklet entitled, "Can Little Children Be Really Saved?" with the sub-title, "Our Task, Which Angels May Covet—A Plea for the Children," and circulated it widely. In this brochure are a number of other stories of children converted in his meetings.

Often skeptics, taking in his penitent-form lined with youngsters, would put the question, "But do the children understand?" Brengle would reply: "I am persuaded that the children often see the way more clearly than their teachers. They see God by faith, find Him not with their heads but their hearts." Even granting the possibility of some not comprehending the meaning of their action, yet "It is not ours to know how far they understand. It is ours to explain the way, and to pray and trust the Lover and Redeemer and Good Shepherd of these little ones to find His way into their hearts. It is well to remember that in inviting them, He said 'Suffer the *little* children to come unto me'—and I think His emphasis was on the word 'little.' "

Heart-warming bits of news came constantly to him from officers who traveled in distant lands where he had campaigned, having left behind him a host of children praying for him. Colonel James Cooke (*R*), of London, wrote one day from Switzerland, years after Brengle had conducted a six weeks' campaign in that country, to say: "Colonel Brengle, the children of Switzerland are still praying for you." Meeting two Scandinavian mothers one day, both told him: "My children have been praying for you every night for years." One young woman officer states that ever since she was four years old, her evening prayer has closed with: "God bless father and mother and Colonel Brengle." In thousands of families the world over, such as that of Brigadier and Mrs. Sam Wood (R), his memory was and is a tower and tradition of holiness; says Mrs. Wood:

While we have no image of him to put up in a niche, still our children through the years of their childhood have looked up to him as to a dearly beloved and highly revered saint. To be "almost as good as Colonel Brengle" was to their minds near the zenith of attainment in spiritual things. Five of them were converted in a meeting for children led by him in the old Memorial Hall, New York City. He preached to the little ones in such a powerful but simple way that even the small tots understood the story of Jesus and salvation. The scene at the penitent-form, as they prayed and were dealt with, was very touching. Before closing the service, the Commissioner asked all the children to pray for him. It was a new thing to our children to have a leader ask for himself the prayers of children, and they joyfully took it up, and continued to do so for many years.

CHAPTER XVIII

TO THE "OUTSIDE"

CONTRIBUTING no little to the sum total of Brengle's work and worth as a preacher was the considerable measure of service he gave to "the outside." By "the outside" is meant the churches, theological schools, denominational colleges and seminaries, summer assemblies, camp-meetings, and the like, where he appeared, not under the auspices of The Salvation Army, but at the direct solicitation of other religious leaders. So eagerly was he sought after for such service that it is safe to assert that, were he a footloose free lance, he could have devoted his entire time to such work.

That he had entrée into the colleges and seminaries, while no doubt due in some degree to his reputation as "one of the most competent and trustworthy guides of the spiritual life of the churches to be found in our country or any other," was due mainly to his scholarship and his pre-Army contact made on their own level with men of the schools. As a college man who was by no means unprominent, this gave him a standing with the educated classes that no amount of godly repute alone could have brought him.

To whatever city in America he might go to conduct a campaign, he met with former college chums, fraternity brothers, seminary classmates. The mere mention of De-Pauw University as his Alma Mater, and the theological

school of Boston University as his place of study for the
ministry, was sure to bring out college men from his own
and all other schools to see him, hear him, and offer to him
the hand of fellowship. It had become, in fact, a matter
occasioning surprise to him to meet with so many who
claimed to have known him at Greencastle, among the
"Dekes," or at Boston.

Through these "outside" contacts he probably won
among the educated more friends and sympathizers for the
spiritual work of The Army than had any of his contemporaries in the organization's ranks. To them he epi-
tomized both the spirit and the message of The Army.

Especially wide was the swath he cut across the affections of the Methodists. As early as July 20, 1892, he
was being made acquainted with a fact that he had not
bargained for when he joined The Army; he wrote with
surprise:

> C—says the Methodists everywhere think a great deal of me.
> Won't it be wonderful, and just like God, if He uses me to bless the
> M. E. Church more through The Army than I could have blessed it
> in its own ranks!!!

Three exclamation points were necessary to carry the
wonder of that eventuality.

One theological school with a platform always opens to
him was the Garrett Biblical Institute, at Evanston, Illinois, one of the three great Methodist seminaries of America. His introduction here came about through his
enduring intimacy with Professor D. A. Hayes.* Hayes
arranged a number of visits for Brengle to the Institute,
as well as presenting him on various occasions to meetings

---

* The classmate in Boston Theological Seminary who was the
first to awaken his interest in Elizabeth Swift.

of the students of Northwestern University, with which
the Institute is connected.

Two other schools at which Brengle conducted revival
meetings and student conferences more or less regularly,
are Asbury College, at Wilmore, Kentucky, and John Fletcher College, at University Park, Iowa.

At DePauw University, of course, Brengle was always
well received. He never, indeed, quite got over his wonder
at the way his name became written across DePauw's sky.
Going to his diary in 1909 he expressed his surprise that—

In a nice letter from Dr. Gobin, vice-president of DePauw, I am
told the university is proud of me as a Salvationist. Why, when I
joined The Army I thought they would almost want to blot my name
off the Alumni Register!

But his surprise reached even greater heights when, on
June 10, 1914, DePauw called him to her chapel to receive
the degree of Doctor of Divinity. Again, upon hearing that
at a reunion of the class of 1883, which numbered many
who had attained eminence in almost every field, it had
been the consensus that "Sam Brengle is the greatest success of our class," he had only smiled his incredulity. But
when he was apprised of the fact that on one Founders and
Benefactors Day at DePauw a renowned speaker had
stated to ringing applause that "the two alumni of DePauw
who are most outstanding in what they have accomplished
for the world's good are Count Chinda, '81, and Commissioner Brengle, '83"—he refused to believe that anyone "could make such a mistake."

And in scores of other institutions of learning his presence was as widely sought. To students and instructors
alike, steeped in metaphysico theological dialectics but
unacquainted with God in a personal way, he often came

as manna to the hungry. Addressing the student body of
Denver University on the occasion of one of his Western
campaigns, he noted that "they are head-full and heart-
hungry":

I am out here at Denver University where there are two or three
professors who were college mates of mine. The Chancellor had me
talk to all the students in the chapel, and then put me into his private
office for an hour to deal with any of them personally who wished to
see me, and I have had a most blessed time. Six young ladies have
just left, most of them in tears. God has been working mightily. He
seemed to help me to get at both professors and students. They seem
to be good and pious, but they need a great shaking up—a Pentecost—to make them what God wants.

Grant University, at Chattanooga, Tennessee, is another school he addressed on occasion; note one result:

God gave me one of the freest times I ever had, and they were all
laughing and crying, from the president down. Afterward, we got
the president down on his knees in his office for sanctification. The
time was too short—a class was waiting for him—to do much, but
I think he got the light. The Lord bless him and help him to walk
in it. He is also editor of their *Southern Advocate*. If he comes out
clearly, he will be a power for God all over this country.

At Emporia, Kansas, he spoke one day to a thousand
fledgling pedagogues of the State Normal School; then,
having to close without making a personal appeal, he told
them: "Come down to the Salvation Army hall; there we
have a penitent-form, and time to use it." A number came,
both to the hall and to the penitent-form.

Wherever he spoke or on whatever topic, he invariably
managed to get in the message God had given him. Having
been asked to speak at a flag-raising at a school in Sioux
City, Iowa, he thus outlined his speech:

I shall tell them that my father died for the flag and that I am
living for it, living in the only way that can possibly bring honor to

it, living righteously—"Righteousness exalteth a nation"—and then I shall pitch into sin, preach repentance, and lift up Jesus as the only Savior from sin and the hope of the individual and the nations of the world.

Given many opportunities of meeting with embryonic preachers and teachers, he seized every occasion to put over a message calculated to bear eternal fruit, not shunning topics that burned in favor of lukewarm and less controversial themes. He wrote on March 14, 1913, from Omaha, Nebraska:

I had a good time at the Presbyterian Seminary yesterday. The president was there, also a professor who is cousin to Mrs. Taft. I didn't know who they were, but I sailed into Higher Criticism, Russellism, and a lot of things, gave my testimony, etc., etc., and I found myself among friends. I preached hell and told them not to throw away their Presbyterian heritage of the doctrine of hell and a whole Bible. How they did sit up! At first they listened—some of them—as though they were inwardly querying, "What will this babbling Salvationist say?" But God let me loose and filled me with a holy jealousy for Him and His Word, and if there was a latitudinarian there, he was not in evidence when I got through. The president, the professor, and a number of the boys expressed their deep gratitude for what I had said. It may reach very far, for some of these young preachers will go to the ends of the earth.

He was frequently asked to speak at preachers' meetings, conferences, and ministerial conventions. Concurrent with a campaign he was conducting in Crookston, Minnesota, the Methodist Conference met, and on October 7, 1900, he addressed the assembled ministers—with striking results. Brengle himself described it thus thirty years later:

The preachers thronged our open-air meetings. Some of them came to the hall and, after hearing me, begged me to come up to their "love feast" on Sunday morning previous to the bishop's sermon, and give my testimony. I accepted their invitation, and they insisted that I go into the pulpit where they could see me. I told them about my conversion in the Methodist Church, my education in Methodist schools, and how God had sanctified my soul and led me into The Army. I was going to sit down, but they pleaded with me to go on, which I did. Just then the presiding elder in whose district the conference was being held, came in, and seeing me in the pulpit, walked quickly down the aisle, saying, "Sit down there, I tell you, sit down!" I can see the old man yet. Peace flowed through my heart like a river. I felt no offense whatever, and replied: "I was just going to sit down, but the brethren requested me to go on, and I shall be through in just a moment." I finished what I had to say, thanked the preachers, and told them I must now hurry down to my own meeting. Many hands were outstretched to me as I passed down the aisle. Some of them, leaving the bishop, followed me to my meeting, and a half dozen or more came to the penitent-form seeking the Blessing. One of them became a flaming evangelist throughout all that region. Several of the preachers said, so others told me later: "We have not believed in the doctrine of sanctification, but that Salvationist has it, else he would never have kept smiling and calm as he did when so rudely told to sit down." I got honey out of the carcass of that lion!

Invitations to conduct revival meetings in churches constantly poured in upon him—from old friends of his Boston days, from preachers who had sampled his message at their own conferences, from those who had attended his Army revivals.

A newspaper in one city where Brengle was advertised for a campaign announced editorially: "If the Apostle Paul himself were to come to this city, it would be no more important an event to the regular churches than is the coming of Colonel Samuel Logan Brengle."

In Ishpeming, Michigan, he conducted a series of meetings for a Methodist minister who was away at conference. As he began the series he expressed this hope in his journal: "I am hoping the Lord will so help us to get the blessing down on them that he [the pastor] will come back and find his church in a revival fire. Lord, grant it!" And that is exactly what the minister did find upon his return.

In Worcester, Massachusetts, taking a service for the pastor of the largest Methodist church in the city—where "the oldest inhabitant could not remember when they had an altar service on Sunday morning in that church"—he had twenty-one out at the altar, and left the pastor with a new-born revival on his hands.

In January, 1927, at the invitation of the late Dr. S. Parkes Cadman, Brengle conducted three meetings in Central Congregational Church, Brooklyn. Writing to him four days previous to the first meeting, Dr. Cadman said:

I want you to give us just the message that God has given you. A revival of true religion, pure and undefiled, is the absolute necessity of the Church in the near future, and you can do nothing better than emphasize the deepening of the spiritual life in believers. I shall leave this entirely to you, because I know you will feel the light of the Spirit of God. We are looking forward to your coming and expect to have a royal time under your leadership.

Brengle's addresses, toned not a whit either up or down, struck fire, and, after the last of the series of sermons had been delivered, Cadman called upon the congregation to pray, dropped on his own knees, prayed most earnestly, and then got to his feet to say fervently to his flock: "Brethren, this is the doctrine and experience and religion that gave us the New Testament and the Church. Without the religion which Commissioner Brengle has preached to us tonight, we should have had no New Testament, no Church!"

Three years later, writing a tribute to his friend, Dr. Cadman said this:

It has been my privilege to know Commissioner Brengle for many years, and during the whole of that period my love and esteem for him have grown from more to more. . . . I am grateful to The Salvation Army for having given him an open door which no man has

been able to shut and an opportunity for a world-wide mission of
evangelization for the saving of souls and the cultivation of the
spiritual life. My contacts with him convinced me of his culture,
both as a true gentleman and as a literary man. His acquaintance
with human nature is profound and sagacious. He knows the Gospel and how it may be applied to various types of character, ranging
from the lowest to the highest in their moral attainments.

In his campaigns Brengle also came into contact with
many of the other celebrated evangelists of his day. With
them he had warmest fellowship; swapping experiences
with them and "talking shop"—if such an expression may
be applied to the industry of soul-winning. Among these
were Dwight L. Moody, Gipsy Smith, G. Campbell Mor-
gan, and J. Wilbur Chapman.

Dr. Chapman, presenting Brengle on one occasion to a
great Los Angeles audience, informed the crowd: "I have
crossed this man's path in all parts of the world; he has a
powerful message." It was on this occasion that Chapman
urged Brengle to accompany him on a contemplated tour
of Australia, an arrangement that was precluded only by
Brengle's already full schedule previously arranged by
headquarters.

A noted missionary, discussing "desirable" evangelists
in a letter to a friend, compared Brengle thus with his
contemporaries:

I have heard many great evangelists of recent time, but Colonel
Brengle of The Salvation Army is no whit behind the greatest of
them. He combines the Biblical scholarship of Torrey, and the simplicity of Dr. A. T. Pierson, with the fervor of Paul Rader—and all
without the slightest trace of sensationalism. He speaks with great
clearness and impressiveness, but in a most quiet, convincing manner. People who miss hearing him will miss an opportunity of a lifetime.

CHAPTER XIX

OFFICERS' COUNSELOR

BACK in the year 1887, a prayer was offered by a young cadet in the Clapton Training Garrison in London with this as its burden:

O Lord, above all things else, make me a blessing to my comrades. I am not anxious for place or name, and if Thou canst better use me to this end at the rear than at the front, I shall rejoice. But let me be a burning and shining light to my comrades!

This prayer Brengle reiterated many times as he came down through the years. It became the dominant theme of his life. While it is true that no one organization could fence in for itself the tremendous vision and influence of such a man, and while it is also true that he became one of The Army's outstanding representatives to the religious world at large, it is nevertheless notable that his paramount ambition was to be "a blessing to my comrades." Just as a man rightly feels that his first duty is to his own family, so Brengle early caught and held the idea that the officers and soldiers of The Army comprised his prime responsibility.

Filled with this one passion—to bless his comrades—he carefully tended the fires in his own heart, "shaking out the clinkers, heaping on more fuel, keeping the drafts open." And because in him they saw the light and felt the glow, his comrades early developed the habit of seeking him out when their fires needed relighting, or of writing to him in the hope that he would dip his pen into the flame of his soul and give just the answer they needed.

Growing consciously lean in their souls, or suddenly discovering the Water of Life leaking out while they had been "cumbered with much serving," they flew to him by letter. And always he found time to write to them at length, answering their questions, leading them back and up. At cheering the disheartened he was especially adept. Mark the tenor of this letter to a prominent comrade who was in the doldrums, having been "tempted to feel useless":

My DEAR TROUBLED COMRADE: "Absolutely useless to God and man!" You must please excuse me for breaking in on your rest with this note, but I'm still laughing and rejoicing—laughing at that ridiculous idea born in your tired brain, and rejoicing to think what a black eye the Devil is likely to get.

You say in your note to me: "I was born to the fight"; and now that you are in a real fight you feel that you are absolutely "useless!" No, no, you have often been on dress parade when you thought you were fighting. When you were at the head of a lot of shouting men and women, cheered by thousands, the Devil may have sat down, crossed his legs and watched it all as a pretty performance. But he is on the job now. I imagine I hear him hiss: "Now I'll crush him! Now I'll smash his helmet of hope! Now I'll rob him of his shield of faith! Now I'll break his sword of the Spirit! Now I'll quench his spirit of prayer;"—and what a Devil he is!

Don't imagine that you are out of the fight. You are in it, and you must fight the good fight of faith now, in loneliness and weakness. But you will triumph.

We Salvationists exalt the active virtues, not too much, but too exclusively. The great battles, the battles that decide our destiny and the destiny of generations yet unborn, are not fought on public platforms, but in lonely hours of the night and in moments of agony.

You were indeed "born to the fight," but do not mistake the nature of the fight. "We wrestle not against flesh and blood. . . . Wherefore take unto you the whole armor of God, that ye may be able to stand in the evil day, and having done all, *to stand*." You can do that, can you not, my comrade?

Said one of Brengle's aides:

The most amazing thing to me as I have watched him through the years has been his inspirational effect upon the lives of Army officers of all ranks. At the International Headquarters in London I have seen the leading Commissioners, engulfed with a thousand duties, set aside their papers, dismiss their stenographers, lock the door, and wait upon the American preacher. They wanted him near, they counted it an event when he visited them, they felt their need of this holy man, and all their actions seemed to say: "It is holy ground. Brengle is here."

That this has been true generally of the entire field of Army officership is apparent to all who have eyes to take in the scope of his influence. He gave himself thoroughly to and for his comrades; and they in turn gave to him an overwhelming abundance of affection and confidence. Always, whether in the front or rear of the march, whether as Cadet or Commissioner, he was to all available, within reach, ready to serve, anxious to bless.

He was especially powerful in officers' councils. Here he did some of his most lasting work. Listening to him, the officers knew they were listening to an authority on the soul, a "spiritual specialist." Most valuable of all is that they felt no gap between them and him. As one put it: "He is a father yet a brother, a leader yet a comrade, a teacher yet a classmate." Among them he never carried himself in a manner likely to foster the feeling that "beyond Brengle, there is no higher experience." Frequently in his letters telling of blessed results in the councils there appear such statements as this:

Such joy, such confession, such heart-searching! It was glorious. *I went to the penitent-form myself!*

The qualities that won him the hearts of his comrades were mainly two: his sympathy and his understanding. A prayer which he set down in his diary one day, lest he forget, was this:

Lord, help me not to be critical of my comrades. Perhaps they are carrying heavier burdens than I. Help me to be sympathetic.

Pleading one day for patience on the part of an officer of high rank who was inclined to be nettled at the dispositions of some of his comrades, Brengle wrote:

You speak of some of our officers who have become irritable. That may be due to rheumatism, to indigestion, to private sorrows. I remember an officer who couldn't get on with any members of his staff. He was testy and cranky, and was much criticized. I was inclined to feel a bit critical of him myself, until one day he opened his heart and told me the cause. He told me of his little daughter who was troubled with a hip disease and heart trouble. He said she suffered torture. Here is his story:

"My wife would spend the day with the little thing in her agony. I would come home at night and find my wife tired out, and I would wait upon the little one and lose sleep. Sometimes the little hip had to be lanced and, because of the weak little heart, anæsthetics could not be used and I had to hold her down by force while the doctor cut into the quivering flesh. Sometimes the pus would spurt out into my face while the little one would struggle and scream in her agony. This continued for years and unnerved me."

As he told me that, a great wave of sympathy swept through my heart and I saw how generous I should be in my judgments of my brethren, and how hesitant to pass judgment upon them. There might be some sorrow, some pain, some perplexity, gnawing at their hearts that I would not understand. "We shall know each other better when the mists are rolled away!"

Young officers particularly sought his counsel. His total lack of rigidity of bearing and stand-offish demeanor made them stand at ease in his presence. They felt free to bring to him any and all of their problems, big and little. Indeed, his letters to the young probably made up the bulk of his correspondence. These contained invaluable spiritual aid. But he also gave counsel on subjects not ordinarily placed in the spiritual category. For example, to a young officer whose zeal had made him unmindful of his health, he wrote:

Take care of your health! Don't let your zeal be quenched in any way, but let it be guided by all the knowledge you can gather, otherwise it might eat you up before it should. Your sword may cut through your scabbard! The body is a near neighbor to the soul and can readily affect the soul. So take care of your health— religiously!

Writing to advise a young woman officer who, scarcely more than a girl, was inclined to be too frivolous for the development of depth of soul, he told her to "Try prayer and fasting—fasting from fun."

He believed, too, in helping to lay securely the foundation-stones leading to the marriage altar. While visiting in the quarters of two young women officers on one occasion, he startled them by asking suddenly if they ever prayed for their future husbands. They laughed, and replied that they did not know whether there would be any future husbands. But Brengle was in dead earnest, and said solemnly: "Girls, somewhere in some part of this world of ours there are two young men whom you may marry. Why not pray that God will keep them clean and pure and upright, away from the things that would drag them down?" Many years later one of these young women wrote to a friend:

Since I have been married, I see the wisdom of that faithful man of God, and thank him often in my heart for the blessing he has been to me in my career as an officer.

If there is one place above another where he delighted to work it was in the Training Colleges for officers. Regularly, over the course of his entire career, he visited annually each of the four such institutions in the United States, and when abroad managed to have included in his itinerary a series of lectures to the cadets of other Training Garrisons.

To the cadets of each session his visit was "the mountain peak experience of the year," as one Training Principal put it. Many of them were his "spiritual children," having been saved or sanctified, or both, in his meetings at their respective corps. Others became acquainted with him through his books. All had heard of him, and looked forward to his visit as one anticipates his Bethel. They read in his battles and temptations and sorrows a saga of their own struggles, and they saw in him the vision and fulfilled promise of a life wholly devoted to one idea.

In the trunk that served him for a file were hundreds of letters, thrust away in a more or less disordered state to await a filing day that would never come. As evidence of the place he occupied in his comrades' estimation, we will quote a paragraph each from only two of these letters, typical as they are of many others. One is from a Brigadier, and was written in 1931:

> I cannot help telling you again, dear Commissioner, as I have told you before, that all through my Christian experience you have come next to God in my life. In my Bible is your picture and under it the question I keep ever before me: "What would Jesus do, and what would Commissioner Brengle do, if they were in my place?" I could never think of you without thinking of Jesus, and I seldom think of Jesus without thinking of you.

The other, written six years earlier, is from one of the most successful young officers on the American field, who signed himself "From a comrade under heavy fire":

> I have just been thinking how I wish I could sit at your feet and feel your hands upon my head, and hear your words of blessing, and

feel the inspiration that God gives through your sainted life. I shall never forget one morning when you called my Lieutenant and myself into your room for prayer, and with your hands placed upon our heads you besought the blessing of the Holy Spirit upon us. That memory lingers in my life, and time will not erase it.

Such, then, is the place in the broad daylight of helpful service that God granted him who was content to abide in dark corners, to march with the lowly in the rear rank, if only he might be, "above all things else, a blessing to my comrades."

Chapter XX

"TONGUES" AND "NEW THEOLOGY"

IN NORWAY a violent reaction to spiritless, formalistic religion took place in 1907, splitting the church asunder, sending one section into the ditch of abnormal emotionalism, and the other into the tangled ravine of subnormal faith. The two radical groups which straightway sprang up, claiming the attention of both the religious and the irreligious, were the Tongues movement, centering in Christiania, and the New Theology movement, with its principal stronghold in Bergen.

Such was the situation that called Brengle again to Scandinavia early in 1907. His function was primarily to establish his own comrades, some of whom had inclined precipitously in either one direction or the other, and, incidentally, to bring back to a sane and normal course as many as possible of the other branches of the Church.

In Christiania he was acclaimed as a deliverer by his comrades and others who had not gone the way of the radicals. He plunged at once into his campaign, and of his first week-end wrote:

Praise the Lord! God has helped us and we had many souls. The big hall was packed last night, and we could hardly close the meeting. I got to bed after midnight. This corps has not been touched by the "Tongues," and seems to be in a very healthy spiritual condition. There are a number of soldiers who got blessed in my meetings last year, and they work and sing and fish like real soldiers.

So quickly did word of his campaign travel that he did not have to go to the leaders of the Tongues movement to study them—they came to him. He found Barrett, the head of the movement,

a hearty, good fellow, but only recently sanctified and in need of guidance. He was a Methodist presiding elder here in Norway, and was elected to the city government before he went to America. He is a musician, an artist, and editor of a paper. He seems to think talking with tongues is the essential evidence that the baptism with the Holy Ghost is received.

The movement as a whole, he discovered, was interwoven with an apparently deep spirit of revival, originating among the Methodists. He found, too, that the teaching was moving in the best of religious company: here was no scattered bit of radicalism among a few illiterate and untaught people; here was delusion on a large and important scale. He saw at once that if he was to correct the error and at the same time rightly direct the prevalent spirit of revival, close study and careful handling would be necessary. He attended one of the movement's meetings to size up the situation, and then wrote down his impressions and conclusions:

One man seemed to be speaking a language. He spoke as naturally as though he were speaking in English and giving a testimony or exhortation. Others were not so natural. One chattered, seemed to be in a trance; one barked out his unintelligible words. I do not think it is a language at all. It seemed to me more like a variety of fragmentary syllables and meaningless sounds repeated over and over. Those affected seemed to be in a trance-like state. There is no joyous light in their faces. I think it is a sort of hypnotic state caused by intense excitement and auto-suggestion. I could not feel the presence of the Spirit in it. It should be avoided: 1. —As not at all helpful to religion, though for the time being attracting attention and leading credulous people to wonder and often to prayer, but likely to cause a sad reaction which would do much harm. 2. —As being very dangerous to the mental and physical, and probably to the final spiritual, health of the subject.

A few days later Brengle was visited by a number of religious leaders of Denmark who were gathered in Christiania to observe or embrace the new teaching, among them being a Brother Rasmussen, of Copenhagen, editor of the then leading evangelical paper of that country. Their visit was presumably for the purpose of discussing the phenomenon of "tongues," but actually it was an attempt to win him over to the new fad. He found them inclined to depend more upon the indefinite than upon the infinite:

I had a good time with them. They have been looking for signs and wonders, and the Lord helped me, I think, to show them the way of faith. How hard it is for people just to believe!

His visitors, however, were not prepared to surrender so readily their new-found faith, with its emotion-stirring capabilities, nor did they relish losing him as a prospective convert. Accordingly, they made a second call upon Brengle, this time coming reinforced with a multi-millionaire merchant and importer of Copenhagen who had been converted in Brengle's meetings in Denmark the year before. With them also were some of the local leaders of the movement. The latter made it plain at once that their principal interest was in propagating the theory of the "gift of tongues" as the main fruit and certain issue of the Holy Spirit's baptism. They even suggested, in all seriousness, that Brengle should get the "gift" and carry it around the world!

His reply to this suggestion discloses how wise was his handling of the situation. Instead of ranting against the error in public or scoffing at their presumptuous proposal, and, by so doing, wounding and alienating a number of sensitive souls, he enlisted their prayers for him, took them to his meeting—and won them from the bogus to the bona-fide:

It was just about time for my afternoon meeting, and I had no time to talk further. But I told them if they thought so, they must pray to the Lord to give me the gift, as I was perfectly willing and wanted all that God wanted me to have. So we prayed, and then they all came to my meeting. I talked on the Holy Spirit and tried to show plainly the distinction between the *Gift* of the Holy Spirit and the *gifts* of the Spirit. Then I spoke on love, and all at once it was as though I had touched an electric button. Nearly the whole congregation threw up their hands and shouted "Amen!" and "Hallelujah!" I told them my own experience, and when I pulled in the net they all came to the penitent-form.

In this spirit of using ardor to overcome error he pushed his campaign forward amid remarkable manifestations. The Brengle holiness tree, laved by the waters of a high tide of interest in spiritual things, bore much fruit. Whereas this city in 1906 had yielded him 226 souls in two weeks, this year the yield was more than 600 for a similar length of time; and in four weeks the numbers of seekers reached 1,017.

It is enlightening to glance at his method of loosing the bonds of the Tongue-tied. Despite his conviction that the error was a result of a "hypnotic state, intense excitement, auto-suggestion," he did not so represent it to the addicts of the doctrine, who would be driven away by such a suggestion. His strategy, rather, was to admit the "gift" to a place among those things promised and bestowed in various periods of the early Church's history—even granting that it may have been given in isolated instances for special service during latter centuries—but showing the while "how insignificant and small is its importance com-

pared with the gift and practice of the great graces: love
and hope and faith." Explaining his method, he said:

I expounded the 12th, 13th and 14th chapters of 1st Corinthians,
laying special emphasis on the 13th, which shows the superiority of
the *graces* of the Spirit over the *gifts* of the Spirit. . . . Many people,
who had been babbling around in tongues, when they heard me came
to the penitent-form for holiness. They saw a great light, and they
didn't indulge in "Tongues" any more. It was swallowed up in a
greater glory and a greater blessing. The Lord is helping me to
show how *practical* the Holy Ghost is.

Sober-minded persons, as well as those whom he had
delivered from the snare, hailed him as their wise guide.
A newspaper editor in Larvik gave prominent space in his
journal to articles about and by Brengle, with prominent
cuts of "the man sent by God to Norway to teach the
people who are religiously hungry, but who are likely to be
switched on to a sidetrack by this talk of 'tongues.'" A
year later, in Denmark, Brengle was visited by Rasmussen, the Copenhagen editor—one of those who had urged
him to get the "gift" and take it around the world—who
embraced him and said: "Colonel Brengle, we are deeply
indebted to you. We no longer feel this movement is of
God. You delivered us from a subtle snare."

Working his way toward Bergen, seat of the other radical departure, Brengle achieved victory in virtually every
town where he campaigned. His spirits were high; neither
did they droop when there came a slump in results at
Fredrikshald, where for several days running he saw but
few at the penitent-form. Instead of complaining, he put
the resultless meetings in God's hands, with the remark:
"He can work backward as well as forward. He can still
bless those meetings and bring much fruit to many souls
out of them. I do believe, and I rejoice in hope." In his

diary he jotted down some good Christian philosophy on this point:

> We are His instruments, and instead of using us to cut a lot of wood just now, He has us on the grindstone, sharpening our faith and brightening our wits and making us cry to Him for help. My soul revels—*by faith*—in the sore discipline. He let Job be stripped of everything, and when He had tried him He gave him double what he had before. God is educating us, and some of His lessons are hard, but by His grace I shall apply myself to them and learn them.

In a few days results appeared. A remarkable "break" came at Drammen. At Arendal the meetings closed with 254 at the penitent-form. At Stavanger, 215. And when Brengle and his aide took the boat for Bergen, their send-off was like that accorded royalty:

> It was estimated that 2,000 people came down to the boat to see us off and bid us God-speed. I have had many people follow me to trains and boats in these lands, but never a crowd like that. I spoke to them from the deck, and they listened as though for life. How my heart went out to them! They want me to come back, but I shall hardly see them again this side of the Great White Throne.

When Brengle reached Bergen, the situation was this: a leading State pastor having adopted the so-called New Theology, with tenets that went quite beyond even that brand of faith termed Modernism, had denied publicly the divinity of Christ, the inspiration and authority of the Scriptures, and other beliefs cherished by the faithful. Orthodox pastors of the city, by way of retaliation, had on several occasions met the heretic in a huge auditorium, and the clash of intellectual combat had been heard. But the exponent of the New Theology, being a man of eloquence, prominent family and extensive learning, had proved a foe hard to rout, and such had been the fine points of the dueling that the man in the street was left as much in the dark as ever. Even the defending pastors were not sure they had carried the day.

Adjutant Westergaard,* the astute corps officer at Bergen, was alive to the opportunity, and had invited Brengle to champion the cause of orthodoxy in the auditorium to which we have referred.

When Brengle entered the hall he saw before him a great crowd of the devout and the intelligentsia of the city: ministers of the Gospel, professors, teachers, editors, lawyers —all wondering, doubtless, just what this foreign Salvationist would contribute to the controversy. On the platform, he took in the character of his audience, fingered a trifle nervously an old envelope on which he had jotted down a few brief notes for reference, and began to wish he had had more time to prepare. He had, however, thought out and prayed over the vital points of his subject, "The Atonement," and when once he was on his feet, all trepidation vanished:

God came upon me. I never felt His presence with me more. My mind worked with perfect clarity. I seemed clothed with the Holy Spirit.

Evidently others thought so, too. For as he spoke the people sat up straight and fastened their eyes on the speaker. Before them they saw a man terribly alive and on fire. Reporters from the local press started to take notes, then forgot that they had pencils. Beside Brengle on the platform stood the Adjutant, who was acting as translator; Westergaard would interpret a sentence, throw it out to the audience, then whisper between his translations: "Beautiful! Give it to them, Colonel!"

* Lt.-Comr. Theodor Westergaard, Terr. Commander, Norway.

And "give it to them" the Colonel did. Beginning his address with a dissertation on sin, he tore off the pretty decorations and disguising labels men have put on it, and revealed it to his audience as the horribly grotesque, leprous, poisonous corruption it is. He opened the covers of history to show sin's ravages, the ruin it had worked on civilizations, empires, families, hearts. He put his hearers in God's place, asked them what disposition they would make of sin, and caused them to understand that all of Omniscience, nothing less, is required if the demands of justice toward sin, and mercy toward the sinner, be met. "God's holiness demands the condemnation of sin; God's love and mercy demand the salvation of the sinner," he hurled, half sternly, half tenderly. Digging far back into beginnings to find the inception of God's plan of atonement, he traced the redemption idea through the ages, and pictured it culminating finally in a Man on a Cross. Was that Man divine? The question now had become all-important, since only divinity, only sinlessness, could atone for sin and save the sinner. "How can we be assured of the Man's divinity?" he asked the crowd, and in the next instant was answering:

The Bible says Jesus is God. Jesus says so, John says so, Paul says so. The Church in all its creeds says so. The wisest Christian teachers say so. The saints and martyrs who have perished by flame and wild beasts' fangs say so. The great soul-winners say so. The humble penitents, rejoicing in the assurance of sins forgiven, say so, and with commingling tears and smiles and heaven-lit faces, cry out with Thomas: "My Lord and my God!"

But [he went on] the testimonies of the Bible and the creeds and the martyrs and the saints and soul-winners and rejoicing penitents do not make me to know that Jesus is the Lord, and I still may doubt. How shall I know? Can I know? A man born blind may hear a thousand testimonies to the beauties of the starry heavens and the glories of sunrise and sunset, and yet doubt it all. Is there any way to destroy his doubts forever? Only one, *and that is to give him his sight. Then he will doubt no more.* He knows. He sees for himself!

Here was evidence that could not be gainsaid, argument that could not be overthrown. The inference was clear without his stating it: deniers of Christ's divinity must be non-possessors of His grace! For, he had made plain, when Christ shall be formed within the heart,

our doubts shall vanish, our sins shall be forgiven, our guilt put away; we shall be born again, born of the Spirit, and have our eyes anointed with spiritual eye-salve, and have our hearts made pure to see God and to discover who Jesus is. And then the Atonement, made by the shedding of His Blood, will no longer be an offence to our imperfect reason and a stone of stumbling to our unbelief, but will be the supreme evidence of God's wisdom and love to our wondering and adoring hearts.

Thus had he drawn a line—the line of experience—between faith and unfaith, showing clearly that the New Theology and its advocates were on the wrong side of that line. His strategy could not have been more perfect. Skillfully, yet without seeming to notice them, he had stripped from his adversaries their qualification to bear arms on a Christian battlefield. Given them rating as Christians, they could have done battle with hauteur and a hearing, but appearing now in the role of unbelievers and strangers to Christ and the testimony of the Holy Spirit, they were in sorry plight.

And when he had delivered his final—

Oh, how He has grown as we have looked! He inhabiteth eternity. The heaven of heavens cannot contain Him. But He stooped to our lowly condition and humbled Himself and suffered and died for us, and made atonement for our sins. And how—oh, how?—shall we escape if we neglect so great salvation!—

the shelling of the New Theology position was complete.

The address over, a prominent publisher rushed to the platform; he wanted the manuscript; he would send it out to all Norway and the world. But all Brengle had was a few scribblings on the back of an old envelope! Mobs of people, big and little, crowded forward to take his hand. One preacher called upon him the next morning to say: "I was so filled with joy I couldn't sleep last night, but spent the night praying and praising God!" Said another, who later was himself to become a noted evangelist in America:

I have heard hundreds of preachers and have seen tens of thousands bow at the altar as a result of preaching, but I have never heard anything like it [the "Atonement" address] fall from the lips of any man. It was the most remarkable testimony to the deity of Christ I have ever heard. Something was fixed that day in my soul. My own doubts flew away. I was established in a new faith. I knew my Lord was divine and I have known it ever since. I have been to the theological seminary and studied evidences of revealed religion, but I never got anything anywhere as I did that night. I shall never forget the great audience. They moved out, not saying how tremendously the rationalists had been answered, but they moved out as if they were saying with Thomas: "My Lord and my God!" The background of that address is in every sermon I preach.

If it is possible to select from a long life-time of preaching any single sermon as the very best in both subject matter and results, the "Atonement" address as given in Bergen, all things considered, may be chosen as the outstanding platform achievement of Brengle's career.

CHAPTER XXI

BEHIND THE SCENES

PREACHING, he lifted high standards. Teaching, he taught high truth. But behind the scenes he lived an even higher life.

If there was any one thing upon which those who knew Brengle agree unanimously more than upon another, it was the close agreement between his preaching and his practice. There was no clash between Brengle in the pulpit and Brengle in private. For if his sermons spoke out loudly on holiness, his own life was yet more voluble on the subject.

A glance at him here and there behind the scenes will serve to explain this harmony.

One of the earliest observations men made concerns his familiarity with the Word. It was impossible to see him in any light, in any place, without becoming conscious of this fact: the man and the Bible are inseparable. His reading of the Book had never been for him simply a dutiful procedure; he went to it as a healthy man seeks his meat and drink, as a scholar delves into his library, as a lover seeks his heart's delight. Not to him was it some "musty parchment," out-moded and dead; it was the Living Word. Its promises became the abutments of his soul, its precepts his guide to action and wisdom, its characters the living companions of all his hours. Consider this:

I am a lonely man, and yet I am not lonely. With my open Bible I live with prophets, priests, and kings; I walk and hold communion

with apostles, saints, and martyrs, and with Jesus, and mine eyes
see the King in His beauty and the land that is afar off. . . . My
daily reading has brought me into company with the great prophets—
Isaiah, Jeremiah, Ezekiel, Hosea, Micah, Malachi, and others—and
I live again with them in the midst of the throbbing, tumultuous,
teeming life of old Jerusalem, Samaria, Egypt, and Babylon. These
prophets are old friends of mine. . . . They have blessed me a
thousand times, kindled in me some of their flaming zeal for righteousness, their scorn of meanness, duplicity, pride, and worldliness,
their jealousy for the living God; their fear for those who forget
God and live as though He were not; their pity for the ignorant, the
erring, the penitent; their anxiety for the future of their people; their
courage in denouncing sin and calling men back to the old paths of
righteousness.*

Of the new Testament characters, Brengle's predilec-
tion was for the apostle Paul. This is not without significance; for, consciously or unconsciously, men describe
themselves best in the characters they esteem the highest.
On one occasion he made this admission:

I am not sure that I lived so intimately with my darling little
wife as I have for many years lived with St. Paul. Far more constantly and intimately than he lived and travelled with his friend
Barnabas and his young Lieutenants, has he lived, travelled, slept,
and talked with me. . . . I think Paul has been my greatest mentor,
my most intimate spiritual guide.

In the Bible, Brengle found pleasure for the mind as
well as pasture for the soul. A man educated to an appreciation of good literature, having browsed long among
the classics and drunk deeply of the productions of writers
ancient and modern—he yet found in the Book of books
the greatest and most engaging literature of all.

I read again this morning [he wrote on May 8, 1912] the story of
Joseph's dealings with his brothers. I can never read it without

* From "Ancient Prophets."

weeping. Why people should go to fiction for thrilling stories when they can read such a story as this, and those of Ruth and David and Esther and Jonah and Daniel, I can't quite understand. Kipling's short stories are utterly chaffy and puerile compared to them. I never think of the Bible stories as literature, but oh, what literature they are! They reveal God.

A habit, formed early in his experience and persisting throughout his life, was his choosing of a "text for today." As a traveller across the desert stuffs morsels of food in his pockets for "munching" and nourishment, Brengle daily stuffed the pockets of his mind with tasty "snacks" from the Word. To these texts—little, short, simple statements of promise, reassurance, comfort—he accustomed himself to turn for support and power along the way. Just crumbs they were, to be sure, but on them his soul grew fat, virile, red-corpuscled. His letters abound in quotations of such bits that blessed him, together with comments that disclosed how appetizing he found them. For example, take this extract from a letter written to Mrs. Brengle in 1896:

My text this A. M. was, "Thy testimonies are my delight and my counselors." The words "my counselors" struck me. The Psalmist sits down and talks over his affairs with God's testimonies and finds out what they have to say. Think of sitting down with Abraham when Lot chooses Sodom and the rich valley; or with Isaac when he surrenders his wells to the Philistines, and talking over the advisability of being meek and yielding to others; or with Job on his ash heap, and talking about trusting God in affliction; or with Paul in the Phillipian jail, and talking about rejoicing in tribulation; or with Joseph or Daniel or David. Bless God! That is just what I do when I sit down to meditate upon and take counsel from God's testimonies.

Most of his Bible reading was done on his knees, he alternating the reading of a passage with the uttering of a prayer; thus God spoke to Brengle and Brengle spoke to God. Through this practice, Bible study and prayer early became for him two forms of devotion inseparably joined.

At prayer, he was a study in communion. It was his habit, except for those periods when he was too ill to get out of bed, to arise between four and five o'clock in the morning and devote at least a full hour before breakfast to communion with his Lord. Dr. Hayes, whose book "The Heights of Christian Devotion" carries these dedicatory words: *"To Commissioner Samuel Logan Brengle, A Man of Prayer,"* gives us this glimpse:

> When Brengle has been a guest in my home I often have found him on his knees with his open Bible on the bed or chair before him, reading his Bible through in that way and saying that the attitude helped him to turn all he read into personal petition: "O Lord, help me to do this, or not to do that. Help me to be like this man, or to avoid this error." A man of simple faith and utter devotion— that is my impression of Commissioner Brengle.

"I had a beautiful time with God this morning!" is one of the expressions that appear often in the Brengle letters. This expression indicates that with him, prayer was not a one-sided bombardment of heaven for the things he wanted; neither was it a mumbled phrasing of formal praise. It was *communion,* wherein he realized God, gained assurance of His presence, satisfied himself of God's pleasure in him. When an interviewer inquired into the manner of his praying, Brengle replied:

> I do a great deal of listening. Prayer, you know, is not meant to be a monologue, but a dialogue. It is communion, a friendly talk. While the Lord communicates with me mainly through His Word, he gives me a great deal of comfort in a direct manner. By "comfort" I do not mean cuddling or coddling, but *assurance*—assurance of His presence with me and His pleasure in my service. It is like the comfort given by a military commander to his soldier or envoy whom

he sends on a difficult mission: "You go, put on your armor, I'm watching you, and I'll send you all the reinforcements you need as they are needed." I have to be comforted that way a great deal. I don't just assume that God is near me and pleased with me; I must have fresh witness to it daily.

Another companion to his devotion, uniting with Bible reading and prayer to form a trinity of ministers to his communion, was the Army songbook. This he frequently referred to as "the modern Book of the Psalms." In 1925 he wrote:

I wake up in the morning, and the patient, silent, watchful, wooing Holy Spirit is brooding over me, waiting to help me to praise God and worship and pray with my waking breath. The Bible and the Army songbook are there to guide my thoughts and my utterance, and when I kneel and open them it is as though I were in a blessed prayer and praise meeting with Moses, Joshua, Samuel, Job, David, Isaiah, Daniel, Jonah, Jeremiah, Matthew, Luke, John, Paul, Peter, Luther, Wesley, the General, the Consul, Watts, Heber, Lawley, and such kindred spirits, and the fire of love kindles and burns in my heart, and my soul soars and shouts and sings for joy. . . . I recommend the songbook for devotional reading!

Systematic tithing, too, was a practice that did its share to keep his communion with God intact. To this habit he had been addicted since his youth:

I tithed every cent of my money even when I was getting my education, and was so poor and in debt that I wore celluloid collars and ate oatmeal almost exclusively. The money I tithed was borrowed. The Devil said: "Here, why do you do this? This is not your money, it belongs to your creditors." I said: "Devil, you're a liar. This is my Father's money; it's only passing through my hands, and He shall have His tenth!" And God prospered me, according to His word. In a remarkably short time, I was able to pay back every cent I owed.

He always fought shy of "investments," believing strongly that "no man that warreth entangleth himself with the affairs of this life." He had not been without temptation here, however: many "opportunities" and "good buys" in real estate had been offered him in exchange for his meager savings. On one occasion, when on the verge of capitulating in California, a text popped up to warn him:

I have been talking to several people today about lots, but I am in doubt about them. I have been warned of danger by that text: "I have bought a piece of ground, and I must needs go and see it: I pray thee have me excused. . . . I say unto you, That none of those men which were bidden shall taste of my supper."

Nothing, no matter how lined with legitimate profit it may have been, was worth while to him if it tended to take his mind from the business of the King. When tempted one day to desire money, just enough to dissolve care and anxiety, the text, "He gave them their desire, but with it leanness of soul," gave him fright. When in Florida during that State's halycon real estate boom, he was bombarded by high-pressure salesmen to buy a piece of property which would almost certainly double in value in a few days, he went to his room, opened his Bible, and saw these words, "O man of God, flee these things."

So wary was he of the enervating effect of wealth that when once it looked as though he and Mrs. Brengle were to be left in legacy a small amount, sufficient to raise his scanty income to a total of about $2,200 a year, his soul went into a flurry of anxiety concerning the imminent "hour of prosperity." One would think, by a reading of the following, that he had been on the verge of taking over the bulk of the Rockefeller millions:

Darling, we must watch and pray, and not be "drowned in perdition," but follow hard "after righteousness, godliness, faith, love, patience, meekness." We shall be fairly rich and the temptation will

be, when we are tired, to settle down and take the world easy. Keep
me stirred up! Don't let me settle down! I must work while it is
day! God has kept us in poverty, and if we walk humbly before
Him, He will keep us in the hour of prosperity—but we must watch
and pray and love and labor and be faithful unto death!

The dire possibility of being overcome with great wealth,
however, was circumvented by the bequest failing to
materialize. And Brengle breathed more easily.

Though he was in every sense a saint, Brengle was not,
in the generally accepted sense of the word, a mystic.
From the time he first began to attract attention as a
preacher of holiness, Brengle discovered he was destined
all his life to be thought austere and unapproachable, until
such time as he could dissipate that impression by personal contact. Even as late as October 4, 1907, he was
found wondering at this attitude. and addressing this question to his diary:

Why are so many people afraid of me before they see me? They
think that holiness makes my eyes like flames of fire, that I will
have no mercy on their infirmities, that they will be searched and
showed up as on the Judgment Day. And when they find out *what a
human creature* I am, that I can laugh and be happy, it is such a
surprise and a relief to them.

About "approachableness" in general he had this to say:

There is nothing about holiness to make people hard and un-
sympathetic and difficult to approach. It is an experience that makes
a man pre-eminently human; it liberates his sympathies, it fills him
with love to all mankind, with compassion for sinners, with kind-
ness and pity for them that are ignorant and out of the way. And
while it makes him stern with himself, it makes him gentle with
others. *It is sin, selfishness, pride, self-conceit, and bad tempers, that
make one hard to approach.* The spirit of Jesus in the heart, which
is the spirit of holiness, makes all men brothers and brotherly.

Typical of the social element of his humanity was his

gentlemanliness; one might even call it courtliness. Those who knew him point to that thing about him which the words "exquisite gentility" but poorly describes, say that he was a compendium of gracious gestures and fine codes, and tell stories of him to emphasize his "high-erected thoughts seated in a heart of courtesy." Colonel Robert Sandall, looking at him with the penetrating gaze of an astute editor and a student of men, once said: "To me, Brengle is the beau ideal of Christian gentlemanliness."

And he was the same with all, high and low, rich and poor. No service rendered him, however small or trifling, got by without a kindly "Thank you!" accompanied by the glowing Brengle smile. Just as there was no toadying to the great, so there was nothing but the gentlest courtesy to the poor. Indeed, one was inclined to think he went to greater pains to ingratiate himself with the lowly- than with the highly-established. A Southern officer tells this:

Entering the Atlanta headquarters building one day, I was approached by the colored elevator boy who had a Bible in his hand. Asking me to pronounce for him a specially long word in a marked passage in a Bible, he told me that Commissioner Brengle had given him the passage to read during the day, with the understanding that he was to report on it in the evening. When I left the elevator, he summed up his impression of the Commissioner's grace in the question: "Ain't he a fine gen'ulmun, though? Why, boss, he even offered to run mah elevator fo' me while ah read!"

Humility, unconscious humility, was another of his traits. He was a skilled user of the soft answer. Such was his spirit that, when caustically criticized, he could rejoin, with an earnestness unalloyed by cant or untinctured with asperity: "From my heart I thank you for your rebuke. I think I deserved it. Will you, my comrade, remember me in prayer?" On one occasion when a person close to him became embittered in soul and sought to vent her spleen by a biting, censorious attack upon his spiritual life, he replied:

I thank you for the criticism of my life. It set me to self-examination and heart-searching and prayer, which always leads me into a deeper sense of my utter dependence upon Jesus for holiness of heart and righteousness in conduct, and into sweeter fellowship with Him through faith in His name.

It was notable also that in him the ostentation of rank found no votary. No matter what rank came his way—and he achieved all in the catalogue of The Army, with the single exception of "General"—men were impressed that here was a man bigger than his insignia. Said a writer in 1930, in apology for having referred to him as "Brengle," with his rank dropped:

There are men to whose name rank and title add weight, prestige; whose position in the minds of their fellows is elevated by it. But not so with Brengle. Rank does not give increase to that name; neither would lack of rank diminish it. In the minds of people the world over, the name *Brengle* means holiness, sweetness, love, benediction, blessing, power; *Commissioner* Brengle means no more. Though the rank he has recently added is a just recognition of his value to The Salvation Army, it is a superfluity in the evaluation of the man himself.

Brengle's own attitude on the question was that of almost total indifference. So uncalculating was he of promotion and its time of arrival, that virtually every elevation in rank came to him as a surprise. On more than one occasion, arriving home vested in a new rank, he forgot to tell Mrs. Brengle of it; and because he was slow to attach his new insignia, she only learned of the event when, weeks later, letters came from headquarters or from friends who used his new title in addressing him. When in later years he was interviewed by a reporter interested in fixing the

dates of various promotions, he had no recollection whatever concerning the when and why of his elevations to
Staff-Captain, Major, and Brigadier.

If he did ever glance rank's way, it was with a sus-
picious eye. He realized that The Army's system demands
promotion for those who are to be its leaders, but he also
saw that the system incorporates within itself serious dangers to spiritual life. Speaking to cadets and young officers,
he warned them:

Don't be in haste for promotion; don't hanker after an easy job.
Promotion may come and find you unprepared for it, and the easy
job will leave you spiritually soft instead of strong and athletic. Hard
work makes strong muscles and healthy bodies, and spiritual hardships develop spiritual athletes. Be content with low rank; endure
hardness as good soldiers. And God will Himself fit you for promotion and leadership.

His greatest fear of rank for himself always lay in the
fact that it might throw a gulf between him and those
"little people" whom it was his passion to serve. When he
received his promotion to the rank of Commissioner,* this
was his first concern, and was the thought he spoke into his
diary:

When people have suggested during the past years that I should
be made a Commissioner, my heart cried out: "O Lord, if the rank
of Commissioner would separate me from the lowest of the low, if it
should cause a trusting or humble soul to shrink in reticence from
me, don't let it come to me!" Now it has come. O Lord, don't let me
lose contact with Thy sheep and lambs!

Yet there was small likelihood that his contact with the
"sheep and lambs" would be lost by nothing more than a
jump to topmost rank. The fact was that no mere insignia,
however dazzling, could keep them from seeing in him the

---

* In 1926.

shepherd who had led them these many years to pastures of rich grazing. To them, regardless of his rank, he was still Brengle—holy, humble, human. His bearing among his comrades, even the lowliest, never seemed to ask for homage. He patronized no man, and expected none to patronize him.

It is not here claimed, however, that he was indifferent to high regard. Occasionally, off by himself, he took an objective look at himself. And he could see the world actually believing the things it said of him, making of him a legend—a legend of greatness, holy greatness. But it is noteworthy that the first thing he saw thereafter was the importance of true humility; better than anyone else he knew how easily topheaviness can throw a man, how an enlarged ego can cause him to stumble and fall. Introduced one evening as "the great Colonel Brengle," he later went to his diary, and this is what he wrote:

If I appear great in their eyes, the Lord is most graciously helping me to see how absolutely nothing I am without Him, and helping to keep little in my own eyes. He does use me. But I am so conscious that *He* uses me, and that it is not of me that the work is done. The axe cannot boast of trees it has cut down. It could do nothing but for the woodsman. He made it, he sharpened it, he used it, and the moment he throws it aside it becomes only old iron. Oh, that I may never lose sight of this! I must continually be humble and recognize the death from which He raised me, the rock from which He hewed me, and the pit from which He digged me.

Looking him over at close range, men saw abiding in Brengle these three: humanity, humility, and—humor. But, to them, the most surprising of these was humor. A story he often chuckled over concerns his sister-in-law, a rather critical young woman who before his marriage to Elizabeth Swift had formed an impression of her sister's suitor that was based simply upon his reputation as a holiness preacher. Seeking to speak before it was too late, she warned her sister one day that as a husband such a man might not be the ideal of congeniality and comfort about the house. But, after meeting him, she rushed to Elizabeth with these words: "It's all right, Lily. He has a twinkle in his eye. He'll do!"

Others made similar discoveries, finding that this man's saintliness sparkled and bubbled with good nature, that his humor was gentle, whimsical, graceful. His smile was the kind that opened suddenly, like a bursting skyrocket; it would start in his eyes, twinkle there, then wreathe and wrinkle over his face, shake his body, and seem to run vitalizingly to his very toes. Those who traveled with him found him the most enjoyable of companions. He had an aptitude for quick wit; he could playfully thrust and parry in verbal sparring matches that he himself liked to promote; he could trade good-humored stories with the best of them. Yet such was the character of his humor that one never thought of it as a temporary departure or excursion from religion; it was part of his religion, good humor in its home atmosphere.

Chapter XXII

"INSTANT OUT OF SEASON"

THE time to take the pulse of a man's interest in his trade or profession or calling is not during "working hours," but after the whistle has blown, the office force has gone, the meeting is closed or not yet started. To be "instant in season" is fealty; but to be "instant out of season" is fervor. In the following incident given in a letter written to his son from Chicago and bearing the date Nov. 18, 1909, we catch a glimpse of Brengle, worker in souls, ever at his job, both in season and out:

I had a fine trip here last night and got the Pullman porter converted at midnight. Passing by the men's room at that hour, I saw him there blacking boots. I asked him about his soul, and found him unsaved. It was a bit cold, but I suggested that we pray. He consented, prayed himself, and trusted in Jesus for salvation, and got up with a new light on his semi-colored face. He said, "I am most grateful to you"—and he looked it. I went to bed and was about to fall asleep when I remembered a little marked Gospel of St. John which I had in my suitcase. I thought, "I'll give him that in the morning." Then I thought, "No, now is the time." So I crawled out of bed, dug it out of my suitcase, and went back to the men's room. He was gone, but his brushes were there, so I dropped it beside them. This morning when he saw me, he said: "I got my Book and I've been reading it, and its alive!"—and again his face shone. He told another porter about our experience together last night, and this one thought it the strangest thing he'd ever heard of—an old man in pajamas at midnight praying with a colored porter! So I left a Gospel for him, too. My man's wife is saved, and he is going home to tell her he has given his heart to Jesus. I think this has given me more joy than all the rest of my campaign—a ton of gold wouldn't have made me so joyful. Hallelujah! A lot of our work will be burned up, George, like hay and stubble, but some of it will abide forever, and I believe that bit last night is one of the things that will abide. I hope to meet that man in heaven. Oh, the joy of winning souls for Him!

Two years later Brengle heard a sequel to the above story. A young woman officer, on her way home to attend the funeral of her mother, was seated one day in a Pullman car, sobbing softly in her grief. A colored porter approached, asking if there was anything he might do for her. The officer told of her bereavement, whereupon the porter consoled her with Scripture quotations and the admonition to "trust and not be afraid." After the officer had calmed somewhat, the porter asked: "Do you know Colonel Brengle, ma'am?" "Oh, yes," replied the officer. "All Salvationists know and love him." "Well," said the porter, "he was the man who prayed with me one night at midnight in the smoking-room. When you see him, give him my love and tell him my wife and I are praying for him daily, and religion is getting better and better in my soul!"

Incidents such as this could be related by the score. No man was ever more consistently about his Heavenly Father's business. This was not, however, because he drove himself to be ever "on the job." Nor was it merely simulated interest. It was perfectly natural with him, the thing to be expected in one whose whole being was suffused with God. Why should he be fluent on the platform, and reticent when away from it? was his attitude. Out of meeting, he talked about spiritual things as naturally as others talk about the weather; more naturally, perhaps, for a man does not have to "make conversation" on a topic which fills his heart and mind; it simply flows out of him.

Why, he asked himself, should he waste time bemoaning

the apparent indifference of the masses to religious things, their failure to attend church and meeting? The masses were all about him, rubbing shoulders with him, on the street, in the cars, in elevators, on ship and train, everywhere. He dropped his seed as he went; he was a wayside sower as well as a cultivator of the furrows.

It often happened, therefore, that many of the souls he won received their blessing—like the colored porter—in the most unlikely places. Sitting in a dentist's chair, he would tackle the dentist while the dentist tackled his teeth. Having conversation with a newspaper reporter, he would take over the questioning, and the interviewed would interview the interviewer. Recuperating at a sanatorium at Dansville, N. Y., he became disturbed about the spiritual condition of those who were treating him, and the doctored began to doctor the doctors. Presented in Miami, Florida, to Count von Luckner, and listening to the celebrated German seaman tell him, seeking to interject a pleasantry, "You know, Commissioner, I am a sort of reserve Lieutenant in The Salvation Army," Brengle replied with a smile: "Is that so? Well, Count, since you are one of us, we'll have to have prayer together," and pulled the surprised nobleman to his knees.

Just as he seldom traveled by train without making an effort to save his Pullman porter, so he seldom entered an elevator without leaving with the operator a cryptic saying to think over; thus:

BRENGLE: "Your life is full of ups and downs, isn't it?"

ELEVATOR OPERATOR: "It is that, sir," smiling.

BRENGLE: "Well, be sure that your last trip is up, won't you?"

A pat on the shoulder and the Salvationist was gone. But the message remained. And many times during the day, and for many days, the operator, while working his lever, would think about that "last trip—up!"

Twenty stories above the crowded main street of Peoria, Illinois, a prominent citizen one day showed Brengle the city—and was himself inducted into a new citizenship in a "City not made with hands." Major James Fookes tells the story:

It was in 1923. Colonel Brengle was conducting revival services at the Peoria Citadel. During his stay there, he also spoke at the Rotary Club on one occasion. Such was the character of the Colonel's address before the Club that the adjutant of the local post of the American Legion, who was also manager of one of the large office buildings in the city, became strongly convicted, but would not yield. He was most gracious, however, and, wishing to do the Colonel a favor, invited him to view the city from the cupola of his building, which was the highest in the city and afforded a splendid view. The invitation was accepted by the Colonel, who enjoyed the view, then began to talk with his host about eternal things. Tears came to the man's eyes under the Colonel's gentle pleading, and in a few minutes the two of them were on their knees, the man finding God and salvation then and there, and turning that isolated spot high above the roar of the city's traffic into a veritable anteroom of Glory.

Since so much of Brengle's time was spent in travel by water, ships afforded him many opportunities for this "out-of-season" work that was always in season. While crossing the ocean on one occasion, he wrote to Mrs. Brengle:

I have one companion in my stateroom. A very nice, easy-going little man, I judge, but I am quite sure he is not saved. Of course, I shall "fish him" clear across the Atlantic. I like him, and hope God will give me his soul.

Another time, while travelling on a coast steamer, he struck up an acquaintance with a distinguished lecturer connected with the Redpath Bureau:

. . . Finally he invited me to his stateroom to listen to one of his lectures, which I did, but I confess with no interest. My heart was bent on getting at his soul. After he was through, I took my Bible and for some time God let me deal with him. He got hungry for a clean heart, and fell on his knees and poured out his soul to God for holiness. How the Lord did bless him! I think he got through.

Another fruitful field for such labors were the homes where he was entertained during his campaigns. "Pray for me, darling," he wrote often to Mrs. Brengle, "that I may be a blessing in my billet." It was not an unusual thing for him, while entertained in the homes of prominent people, to win the entire household to Christ. Never, in any case, did he leave a billet without having brought all within the house under the consciousness of his passion. This he would do so tactfully and gracefully that it was never offensive; no more so, indeed, than the polite presentation of one's best Friend would be anywhere offensive to one's host or hostess.

Upon learning he was to be in the city, Christian families of high degree especially were wont to bid for his presence in their homes. A certain aristocratic lady in Holland, after having entertained him during his visit to that country, summed up the meaning and fruit of his stay there by saying to Mrs. Commissioner Estill: "Oh, that blessed blessing of a man! Can you not bring him back?"

In no place was his gift for adding spiritual atmosphere better evidenced than at the table. His was the art of so artfully directing the channels of tabletalk that he could turn an ordinary meal into an informal service of communion. On the occasion of one of his visits to DePauw University, a Roman Catholic woman sat at the table with him, and when the meal was over she went to her friends to say: "It seems as though we have been talking with God." The tribute of Major Wesley Bouterse, who for years traveled with Brengle and watched his influence on all kinds of crowds and places, is this:

> If he did no public meetings, I believe Commissioner Brengle's life, because of his personal dealing with people behind the scenes, would yet be more fruitful than that of most of his contemporaries. It is my opinion that he does nearly as much good across the table with friends as he does in meetings.

One of the tenderest epics of out-of-season work to be found in any account, outside of the Bible, is a narrative Brengle himself has told of his dealing with a young girl of a theatrical troupe whom he met on a train. In addition to being a poem in tactful, sympathetic, personal dealing, the following narrative gives us what is perhaps our clearest glimpse into the compassionate soul of the narrator:

> As usual, the girls of the troupe were pretty, painted little things, with pencilled eyebrows and lashes, bizarre-dressed, and, of course, they were "hail-fellow-well-met" with all the men of their party. . . . It was a troupe of theatrical people, who, with the exception of another gentleman and myself, filled the sleeper in which I was to cross New Mexico on a recent journey. My heart was a bit heavy and cast down when I looked at them and listened to their empty chatter; there was nothing in common between us, so it seemed to me, but I found my heart going out with pity and sympathy toward the young things who seemed so pathetic in their spiritual poverty and ignorance of all the high and true and lasting values of life.
>
> When the porter began to make up the berths for the night, one of the older girls, waiting, sat on the arm of one of the seats of my berth. I removed my coat and begged her to sit down. At first she hesitated—possibly she felt the lack of common interest as much as I—for she saw me in full uniform. For a few moments we sat opposite each other in silence, while she watched in rather a grave way what appeared to be a furious flirtation going on across the aisle.
>
> I wanted to speak to her, but hardly knew how to begin; at last, however, I made some common-place remark about the desert through which we were passing . . . and soon we were in conversation. I asked her about her work, and she told me of the long hours

they spent in play and rehearsal—from ten to twelve every day—a matinee in the afternoon, and play again from 7:30 to 11:30, never getting to bed before 1 A. M. And I noticed that, beneath the camouflage of paint and powder and wild profusion of golden hair, she looked tired and, I thought, a bit world-weary and disappointed. I asked her if she didn't miss home life, and she told me she had a good home in Chicago, but that she got restless after spending two or three weeks there, and then must go on the road again.

I told her that I understood, and that I was sure that this restlessness would grow and become more and more consuming, and that I knew of but one cure—that of which old St. Augustine wrote: "Thou, O God, hast made us for Thyself, and we are restless till we rest in Thee!" I told her that our souls were too great to be satisfied with anything less than God Himself, and that He is the rightful home and great Comrade and Friend of the soul. I told her that when I was a little orphan boy, made so through the death of my father, it was not the four walls of the house that made my home, but mother herself. She was the home of my little child-soul; but by and by she, too, died, and then my soul found its true rest and rightful home in God, in fellowship and union and sweet and tender friendship with Him.

I told her of Jesus, and His great love and sacrifice for us all, and she listened—oh, so quietly and intently!—and then she arose and gave me her hand in an eager and warm clasp, and, looking deep into my eyes, thanked me with an earnestness that made me forget the paint and powder—for her soul was looking direct at mine—and then she was gone. But an indescribable sweetness filled my heart. I felt the presence of Jesus, as when He was upon earth, still seeking the lost to save them. And then I realized, it seemed as never before, how He was the Friend of sinners; how He loved them and longed for them; and that night He gave me a fresh baptism of love for the lost, the wayward, the straying, the befooled souls who are trying to find satisfaction without Him.

At three o'clock in the morning, in the stillness and darkness, that weary troupe of players slipped out of the train so silently that I did not hear them go, and I may never see them again, but my soul has been sweetened by the chance meeting with them. The quiet talk with the girl, who is beginning to be disillusioned and to feel the vanity of all things without Christ, left a blessing in my soul that will abide, and in the strength of which I shall go for many days.

Looking at that scene, one can easily imagine the picture of the man and the uniform and the train and the girl fading from the canvas, and in its place see pictured a vision of Another, talking quietly and simply beside a well to a woman from Samaria.

Like his Master, Brengle was "instant," both in and out of season.

Chapter XXIII

HUSBAND

THE literature of all time would be hard driven to produce record of a more idyllic marriage than that of Samuel and Elizabeth Brengle.

There was an occasion shortly after their wedding when Mrs. Brengle, entering a bookstore for the purpose of purchasing Tolstoy's *"What I Believe,"* was given instead the only work by that author which the store had in stock. She held the book in her hand, turned it over, read the title. It was *"Anna Karénina"*; a day or so later she wrote her husband:

While the clerk hunted a price list I looked at the book. I didn't know the names of Tolstoy's novels, and this might be philosophical for aught the Russian title meant to me. But it was a novel. I opened to the last pages where a woman's husband was talking to her, explaining that that phase of their love was over, that it was in the course of nature and could never return. They walked on to the house and her little children were brought out to her, and she was satisfied; she kissed them all with a sort of fury, and the child-love made up to her for the other which had lived its day. I put down the book, but as I walked home I was wild to buy it. I didn't care for the story, but what phase of married love was it which must die a natural death while the lovers still lived on? I wanted so to know. I looked in memory at your love; there isn't one bit of it that I can spare, that I can bear to lose, or have change. But if I must, why not let Tolstoy tell me and prepare my mind?

But I just took the matter to Jesus and He showed me that the man who wrote Tolstoy's novels was not then saved and knew nothing of any love in Christ. But it was hard even then to rest *satisfied*.

202

I didn't want the novel, only the information, and the temptation was strong and keen. But after a little I got peace, became quite content to leave your love where I found it—in God's keeping. What happens to it there, will be good for it and for me, and I shall like it even to be changed, if He wills it so.

In that last sentence is there not just a suggestion that perhaps God might allow such a "natural death" to love while "the lovers still live on"? That perhaps Tolstoy, his unconverted condition notwithstanding, might have been right in his characterization of life which, however bitter, was after all—life? The tone is more of the spirit of resignation to what may be the inevitable than the satisfied conclusion that such a condition could only exist in perverted love.

So did the chief character of Tolstoy's novel pause for a moment before Brengle's bride, whisper disturbing thoughts in her heart, and give to this couple a hint of unChristian philosophy which it would be theirs to more thoroughly disprove than almost any other wedded man and woman. All their life together they both were to remember the foolish fear that she here allowed to grip her for a moment but as quickly hid in God, and they would laugh at it and rejoice together in a union which tenderness, constancy, undying affection, self-sacrifice and holy companionship would weave into one of the most beautiful patterns found in any story of marital bliss.

But as the years passed, and they grew more and more into a perfect union, Brengle did not let her forget her experience with Tolstoy, and would periodically tease her with: "Now don't you see what a foolish little woman you were to allow him to distress you?"

Not once, from the time he had sat in the church in Boston and heard and seen her for the first time, did the suggestion of a doubt cross his mind that she was his

"God-given wife." As such she proved to be an epitome of all that is contained in the word "helpmeet." "How good God was to give you to me!" is an expression he never seemed to tire of making.

Theirs was a marriage in which real communion of soul existed to a marked degree. When it happened one day that she prayed and he preached from the same text at the same hour, he wrote jubilantly:

He gave you my text! And as you prayed His power came down and thirty-six were saved at the penitent-form. Bless the Lord! I have just told O—, and he laughs and says, "Spiritual communion! Wireless telepathy." Amen! I believe in the Holy Ghost, and the *communion of saints!*

With perfect candor, they told each other of their spiritual conflicts and victories. They made a practice of testifying to each other in almost every letter; and when once she failed to do this, he wrote back with a tinge of anxiety showing in the ink: "You didn't testify in your letter, darling. Is it well in your soul just now?"

Even in the matter of reproving and rebuking each other, they were not slack. An example of how he sought from the first to place himself and Mrs. Brengle in the sunny realm of utter frankness where each would be the free-spoken guardian of the other's soul, is seen in the following, written from Clapton:

My OWN LOVE: I hope you will never have occasion to do so, but if you ever do, don't hesitate to plunge God's sword clean through me. Do it for His sake, for your own sake, and for mine.

When once she had pulled him up on a matter, he wrote in his next letter: "I do thank God that you were faithful to reprove me!" Always he encouraged her to "keep me stirred up, darling":

Help me by your prayers, stir me up by your exhortations, make me watchful by your warnings, make me diligent by your example, make me wise by your counsel, be my wife, my helpmeet, as you have been and as you will—and God will use me to save many more souls with you than without you.

It is noticeable, too, that while he was going forward, growing in grace and ability, she would not allow her rather circumscribed sphere to cause her to lag behind. In one letter she adjured him thus:

I am glad that you are going in for deeper things, my beloved. My heart goes with you. I must keep pace with you spiritually, or lose sight of you in Eternity. Always urge me on, my own darling, and don't let me stay lagging behind.

As these two became more and more in love, Tolstoy and his *"Karénina"* suffered ignominiously in every letter passing between them. Each bit of correspondence contained its constantly iterated but freshly expressed portion to remind each other that the flames of love had not died on the hearthstone of the years. Nowhere in their love-life can one find a trace of that frigid, bored, take-it-for-granted, careless, forgetful brand of affection. They loved, and they expressed that love to each other freely and often. Devoted, they did not fail to let that devotion speak itself out in tender expressions, thoughtful care of each other, and close attention to the "tremendous trifles" of married life.

Brengle as a lover was nothing if not enthusiastic. In one of his early letters to her, he had styled himself "the fondest husband in America," and from then on proceeded forthwith to prove it. The thought of her was as the turn of a tap: what was within poured forth in a sparkling, spontaneous rush. See in the following his love running riot:

See here, Mrs. Lily Swift Samuel Logan Brengle, I love you till I hardly know what to do with myself! I'm awfully in love, hopelessly in love, head over heels in love, and altogether in love. No help for me! I never expect to get over it. I'm swallowed alive and whole in love—engulfed deep, no way of escape—overpowered, enveloped, and buried in love. There's my latest autobiography. That's the heart of it!

Now and then his extravagance in expression flowered out in even more imaginative luxuriance. Note this:

I'm in love. If that is an old story, so stale that you'd like me to cut it out, maybe by some superhuman effort or divine interposition I could do so, but it's true all the same. I'd like to get out on top of this hotel and shout it till you could hear it in Amenia [he was writing from Grand Forks, North Dakota!]. Wouldn't that be fine? and wouldn't it surprise a lot of folks between here and there? What a commotion and hub-bub it would set all the surrounding states and Canada into. It would reverberate from the Rocky Mountains and peal over the Alleghenies and wake up the Mississippi Valley and startle Chicago and hush New York, and be a nine-day's wonder that would make people forget Roosevelt's boom and the Chinese Revolution for the space of half an hour, I'm sure. There now! You know how I feel.

Writing his letter to her at times with a blue pencil, when he came to say "I love you!" he would pick up a red pencil and scrawl the declaration all over the page, putting after it a long series of exclamation marks to add emphasis. Usually he wrote his letters to her by hand, but now and then when dictating other correspondence he would dictate one also to her, reserving, however, the love expressions for his own writing, and saying: "As my stenographer is an old maid, I'd better write the love part in my own hand." Sometimes in the thick of the fight, having no time for a full letter, he would, nevertheless, take the time to excuse himself and, drawing a card from his pocket, would fill it with the capital letters of an ab-

breviated code he used for expressing his love, and make
the notation in one corner:

I am surrounded by folks, so I abbreviate. But there is no abbrevi-
ation of my L. That flows on in a torrent—deepening, widening,
day by day!

During his illness in Denmark, unable himself to write,
he authorized his aide to send the following:

The Colonel has just given me these capitals as a personal message
from him—I.L.Y.W.A.M.H.Y.S.S.L.W.O.M.

The writer himself might have been mystified, but the one
to whom the letter went had no trouble translating the
capital letters into: "I love you with all my heart, you
sweet, sweet Lily—wife of mine."

"He hath made them one flesh" is a verse that aptly
describes Brengle and his wife, and suggests a closeness,
a union, a communion, that no amount of mileage could
destroy. And though of these separations—the heaviest
cross they both were called upon to bear—she could say:
"I feel bisected; my body is here, but my heart is away
with you," she nevertheless would not have had it otherwise, and could also say:

I exult in the great work God is doing through you, and rejoice in
the privilege of making a great sacrifice for it. I love you just as
much a hemisphere away, and perhaps a little more, because I
realize your worth so keenly in absence.

And though she felt keenly the sacrifice of it all, she never
conceived of herself as a martyr, for "even if He does
borrow you pretty often, you are really His first, and I
have you in Him."

Cropping up in almost every letter he wrote to his wife
during their separation, were traces of his longing for
her. Here is a sample:

My precious, precious one, I love you. Every day I long for you more, and have to silence the clamor of my heart by absolutely refusing to think of the long weeks of separation and by staying my mind on God and His great soul-saving efforts. It would be so easy for intolerable pain to fill my heart if only I were to dwell at length upon my inability to take you in my arms. . . . Sometimes I have to turn to the dear Lord quickly, to save me from the swift impulse to pack up and sail for America at once. I can and will wait, my darling, but sometimes the thought amounts almost to pain.

In the following we can sound a yet deeper depth of their devotion first to God, then to each other:

Do you remember that morning when you said that for His sake you would be willing for us to part and never see each other again? To that I could say, Amen. Then you added, "Yes, for the salvation of *one soul* I would be willing never to see you again." That word convicted me. I knew that to follow Jesus meant just such a consecration, and yet I didn't feel that measureless love in my soul that could make me say it. . . . I could only say "Thy will be done," not gladly, but with full purpose not to shun the cross. Since then, in the last few days, the dear Lord has been filling me with His own fulness of love for the poor sheep for whom He died, so that I can say, "All things I forego, my King, for one precious soul." My own sweet Lily, I love you none the less, but rather much more, as I love Him and them more fully.

Such, then, was the thorough, glad surrender this couple had made to the claims of the Gospel—a surrender before which the carnal world stands uncomprehending and shakes its head. To them, their early-adopted motto "God first!" meant just that—with no reservations.

May 19th, their wedding anniversary, was always a time for the exchange of tender thoughts. And though on many anniversaries he was in one part of the world and she in another, the day was always observed in their hearts and letters. The thought that heaven was actually where their marriage originated was never doubted, but grew stronger with the years. When she sat down in 1906 to address her

anniversary letter to him in far-away Denmark, she wrote:
"This is the day that the Lord hath made!"—but hastened
to add:

Yet, I will tell you privately that I would not exchange any day
with you now for our wedding day. *Any common day,* when we're
tired, and things go wrong and the world seems very grubby, *is better
than that day, wonderful as it was.* Other people might think that I
was depreciating that day. But you won't. I mean that you are so
much sweeter and dearer and more lovable that I wouldn't go back
to that feeble day of possession in that faroff time. May 19th was
an excellent foundation for the better days that have followed.

On the same day he penned this:

Nineteen years ago today we were surrounded by sweet flowers
and friends, and you became my wife. Oh, how I love you and how I
wish I could tell you how sweet and dear you are to me. You have
gone on increasing in sweetness with every passing year. You have
filled my heart with joy and peace. . . . I have been praying the
Lord, if it please Him, to give us another nineteen years, but I don't
see how they can be more wonderful than those of the past.

And as always, on the anniversaries particularly, Tolstoy
came in for his annual rap for his slight on the possibilities
of extended bliss in the marriage state, as revealed through
"Anna Karénina." This time Brengle gently chided her
thus:

What a misguided and misguiding old fellow Tolstoy is! Do you
think you have sufficiently repented for listening to him?

CHAPTER XXIV

HEALTH AND UNHEALTH

As HIS day grew long and approached its late afternoon,
Brengle had a saying:

Manifold trials call for manifold grace; manifold grace works for
us manifold experience; manifold experience gives us a manifold
testimony, enabling us to meet manifold needs.

In such a statement he summed up his mature philosophy on physical suffering and its relation to the Christian
economy. Written in his own body were the marks of
much pain; but these he did not regard as the scars of
sin. They were the signs of fellowship with his Lord in
toil and suffering, and passwords that gave him entry into
sorrowing and burdened hearts the world over.

Brengle, while never doubting for a moment God's
ability and willingness to heal bodily ailments, was not of
that school which declares all sickness and infirmity to be
closely related to sin, and hence outside of God's purpose
and will. To him, the granting of God's sustaining grace
was an even more impressive miracle than was the application of His healing power. And, so far from seeing in
manifold afflictions signs of God's displeasure, he read
therein his Lord's mark of favor. He often said:

God does not make pets of His people, and especially of those
whom He woos and wins into close fellowship with Himself, and
fits and crowns for great and high service. His greatest servants have
often been the greatest sufferers.

210

It appeared to those who watched Brengle that his physical condition was a matter of extremes: he was either very well or very unwell. This, however, was not because he never occupied that distressing middle ground between blooming health and blasting unhealth; that he appeared so was because he never allowed himself to give in until completely overcome, but would laugh away all minor complaints as mere trifles, maintaining a happy, buoyant spirit until some malady positively forced him to bed. His spirit drilled his body into an habitually erect and optimistic carriage which could be forced to drop but could not be induced to droop.

Early in his experience he learned the importance of the care of his body: "I found that I have the treasure of the Lord in an earthen vessel, and that I must behave myself if I am to be physically happy and efficient."

Had he not taken such care of his body, it would not have stood up to a tithe of the tasks he forced it to perform. He maintained a systematized order of living with reference to food, clothing, personal habits; all his life he practised daily—when able to be on his feet—a routine of exercises known as the "Delsarte gymnastics." To this regimen he attributed his usual vigor and state of well-being.

Of what then, when he spoke of "manifold trials," was he thinking? What was behind the saying?

Sicknesses, ailments, abrasions, accidents—in severity and number far above those which visit the average man in his lifetime—came to him. His had not been a single thorn in the flesh, buffeting him with repeated attacks; rather had he felt the pricks of an infinite variety of thistles. He could think, for example, of these:

The injury to his head wrought by the Boston tough's brick (from which he never altogether recovered).

The scores of illnesses brought on by exposure, by his exhaustive labors and wearying travels, and by preaching in crowded and ill-ventilated little halls when scarcely able to keep to his feet. His undergoing three major operations and many minor ones. Teeth troubles that took him into dental parlors in many lands, enabling him to remark: "I could get up a most comprehensive and authoritative dental directory of the world!" The agonizing and dangerous malady (rheumatic fever) which took him close to death's door when in Denmark in 1908. Stubborn ailments of one kind and another which he kept under only by the most careful attention to diet, exercise and self-doctoring. And, on top of all these, a shocking automobile accident which, coming upon him at the age of sixty-four, swept him nearer the River than he had ever been before.

Looking at his life, in which the elements of health and unhealth were so strangely apportioned, the above-mentioned may be some of the things basing his thought when he used the words, "manifold trials."

More interesting, however, than the fact that such trials came to him, is the question: How did they leave him?

It is not too much to say that, in looking at his manifold sufferings and trials, we are looking at the things which largely made him Brengle. When a newspaper reporter interviewed him in Lake Charles, La., among the things Brengle told him was this:

I am a constant student in God's school, the University of Hard Knocks. I have forgotten much that I learned in two universities, much of the Latin, the Greek, and the Hebrew. But I will never forget the lessons I have learned in God's school. It is there that moral fibre is developed. When I get to heaven I'm not going to ask Daniel how many featherbeds he slept upon in Babylon, but I am anxious to ask him about the night he spent in the lions' den. And the first thing I am going to ask Paul is about the shipwreck, and the times he spent in prison. It takes these things to make a man.

Again and again when sickness interposed itself, cutting athwart his plans, checkmating his moves, he would still his soul into quietness by anticipating God's greater glory through the trial. During one particularly long period of ill-health, he copied into his diary many comfort-verses; one of them was this:

> Be quiet; why this anxious heed
> About thy tangled ways?
> God knows them all. He giveth speed—
> *And He allows delays.*

Under the last line he drew an underscore for emphasis.

No claim is here made, however, that all his life Brengle stood with arms outspread to welcome such physical trials as rendered him impotent of action. Crosses they were—every one of them—which, placed upon his shoulders, weighed him down with depression of spirit. Often at the time of his visitation he was unable, despite the most earnest scrutiny, to see in some of his experiences anything even remotely suggestive of the hand of God. Then would come a battle with his feelings, with the descent upon his mind of a constitutional melancholia with which he had had to fight ever since the brick incident and which was ever wont to grip him when his days were less resplendent.

He knew frequently the exhaustion of spirit that is often conjoined with exhaustion of physique. Time and again, in the heart of some arduous campaign, his body would cry out to be spared, and his soul's almost spontaneous reply was, Amen. Times without number his faith would be forced out on the midnight battlefield to contend for its very life. Victory was not easy. Is it any wonder that he, who during his whole career had been normally active in pursuing the burning passion of his soul, should find it difficult to become habituated to suffering and suffering's hand of restraint?

At such times his "strong tower" was to trust, to cling blindly to God. While not always possessing the prescience to foresee God's purpose, he had the Presence to fortify his faith. And later, when viewed in perspective, the trials invariably had a way of assuming the form of instruments of grace. An example of his method of victory is seen in a diary entry made during one period of convalescence:

Am slowly regaining my strength and nerve following my recent operation. It was trying beyond measure. My appetite failed, my blood became thin, impoverished, my brain was under-nourished, my nerves were ragged, frazzled, exhausted, and such gloom and depression fell upon me as I had never known, although depression is an old acquaintance of mine. God *seemed* non-existent. The grave seemed my endless goal. Life lost all its glory, charm, and meaning. But God has delivered me. Prayer brought me no relief; indeed, I seemed to have lost the spirit of prayer and the power to pray. Then I remembered to give thanks and praise God, though I felt no spirit of praise and thanksgiving. Feeling, except that of utter depression and gloom, was gone. But as I thanked God for the trial it began to turn to blessing. Light glimmered, grew slowly, and then broke through the gloom. The depression passed away, and life was beautiful and desirable and full of gracious incoming once more. Hallelujah!

In such a manner it was his habit to take hold of every dark disappointment, every stabbing pain, every confining infirmity, and, like men take hold of an oyster, break it open and extract from it a resplendent pearl of priceless blessing.

Something else which his sufferings had discovered to him was "what a glorious brotherhood is the secret order of the sons of God!" The extremely high place he held in the affections of his Salvationist comrades, and in the hearts of innumerable Christians outside The Army, was evidenced by the flood of mail that poured in upon him whenever word went out regarding his ill health, the necessity for an operation, or some untoward accident. Such letters were sent from all points of the compass, bringing back to him a measure of the comfort and assurance of prayer that he himself had given out at various times to the letter-writers. Truly, the return of "bread cast upon the waters."

Most valuable of all the assets his physical sufferings added to him, however, was the new understanding of, and new entrée to, the hearts of those who otherwise could not have been reached by him. With the passing of each of the "manifold trials," he invariably found that it left in his hand "another key to the hearts of my fellows." And so varied and numerous were his experiences that his keys were many.

Thus, through the years, the "eternal weight of glory" increased for Brengle as a result of his "manifold trials." Every troubled soul who had found comfort and health in his experience, every ailing one to whom his life had added faith and fortitude, every person who had been inspired by his example to bend his back more cheerfully to his cross—all had added daily to the abundance of this man's "glory." Because he gloried in (not *for*, as he sometimes pointed out) his infirmities, the power of Christ rested strong upon him.

"Most gladly, therefore, will I rather glory in my infirmities." It was the Apostle Paul's word. But Brengle caught it up and relayed it to his generation. It was a victorious note. It was a cry from the ramparts of the unconquerable.

Chapter XXV

"VANISHED HAND"

It was in March in 1915. Winter had lingered late, as though reluctant to make way for the softer solicitudes of spring. In New York City snow thickly carpeted the streets, while against the windows of the hospital hail beat its dismal staccato like droppings from lead-painted skies.

Motionless on a cot lay Brengle, measuring the march of the weary hours. The great wound in his body that marked the recent path of the surgeon's knife protested the necessity of his breathing, protested with pain that advanced and receded with the rise and fall of his breath, stabbingly rhythmical.

In those rare periods when the pain was not too severe, his mind could reflect upon the tragic series of trials which had afflicted him during the previous few months. He could think, with a degree of disappointment, of his unexpected appointment to the principalship of the New York Training College—of the delightful hope it had brought of having at last a degree of home-life, a welcome recess from travels and separations—of his installation by the Commander. Then, in the midst of the installation ceremony, the shooting pain and agony which had wrung from him the all-too-accurate prophecy that his "next appointment will likely be the surgeon's table"; the major operation that had followed, and the uncertain recovery necessitating another prolonged stay at the hospital; Mrs.

Brengle's sudden and complete breakdown at this point, and her removal to a sanatorium; his anxiety over her condition, and his finally leaving the hospital to go to her; the development of another condition in himself that called for a second major operation; and now this great hole in his body, this hovering so near the River, this impotence which made it impossible for him to be by the side of her who so sorely needed him.

He felt tired, worn, an instrument played out. Had not the Master compassed every tune, tone, and tempo on this instrument of His? From this life, had He not sounded all heights and depths of human emotion and agony for His greater, though inscrutable, glory? True, this was the same instrument which from a fever-tossed bed in Denmark asked the question: "Is there not a great harmony in pain?"

Yet even harmonies are exhaustible; what other could this instrument give? Howbeit, the Master knew His instrument. There was yet one other harmony—if harmony it can be called—deeper, more poignant, than any yet experienced. The fingers of the Master's hand sought a minor key position on the frets. . . .

One day the surgeon entered the room, wearing the expression of a bearer of ill tidings. Seating himself by Brengle's bed, the man whose business it was to wound people found it awkward to use words. Then—

"Colonel, your boy is downstairs with a message. He says he cannot face you with it, and asked me to give it to you. A telegram has come. Your little wife is dying."

Afterwards, Brengle thus described the feelings which then broke the dikes and flooded the bottom-lands of his soul:

A thousand times, in distant lands and lonely hours, I have been stabbed by the thought that possibly my darling might die before I could cross oceans and continents and reach her side. Now, lying only a hundred miles away, she was dying—and I was at the point of death and couldn't go to her. It seemed as though my heart would break, and it seemed as though God didn't care if my heart did break. But I did not go by appearances. I had preached all round the world that God *does* care, that all things do work together for good to them that love the Lord, and I didn't cast away my confidence and charge God foolishly. I was very weak, but I took my Bible and songbook and I read the promises and nestled down upon them, and I read the hymns of comfort and guidance and heaven and I nestled down into the will of God. I said, "O Lord, Thou knowest how I love my darling and how desolate I shall be if Thou dost take her, but I don't know what is best for her or for the dear children or for myself. Thy will be done." And peace entered my heart.

In three weeks he, whose calling had afforded him such comparatively short periods of her companionship, was allowed to leave his bed and, in great weakness and pain and weariness, go to his wife's side to be near her in her last earthly hours. For days he watched over her—praying, quoting Scripture, softly reciting verses of hymns, their old favorites. A poem he repeated often was one of her own, written to be sung to the tune, "The Rosary"; its last verse has these lines:

And when my day on earth is done,
  Heaven's morning breaks and shadows flee,
When just before me waits Thy Judgment Throne,
  Earth's last dread hour I'll spend, my Lord, with Thee.

A few days before the end came, her circulation became so feeble that her hands swelled, making it necessary to cut off their wedding ring. And when the jeweler removed the circlet, symbol of the tender love and union of twenty-eight years, the inside revealed an inscription Brengle had had engraved there many years ago: *"Holiness unto the Lord."* Their motto, their covenant, their pledge to one another, still speaking in "this last dread hour."

To a friend in London he wrote:

My heart rests in His will, and is comforted even while it is torn. . . . If He takes her I shall not lose her. Her mind wanders at times and she may not be able to recognize me, but if I ask her, "Is Jesus with you, darling?" instantly she responds, "Yes, indeed, praise the Lord, He is in our hearts." She never loses herself on that point.

On Saturday, April 3rd, it became plain that the end was nigh. Throughout the day she sank rapidly, unable to speak or respond in any way to anything said to her. Brengle—having the thought that possibly beneath the apparent unconsciousness there might be a spirit consciousness—susceptible even now to the Devil who might be following her down to the very gates of death, assailing her faith, fighting for her soul—spent hours bending over her form, quoting promises, their old beloved "texts," to encourage her faith if perchance she could hear. At last, at three o'clock when he bent over to repeat the question: "Are you trusting Jesus, darling?", this time, ever so faintly, hardly articulate yet unmistakable, as from a great distance made greater as the earth was receding, she made answer to this last challenge for her testimony: "Yes!"

It was her last word. In less than a half hour, the end came peacefully. When he sought to write of it a few days later, he said:

She fell asleep in Jesus as peacefully and unafraid as ever her tired babies fell asleep in her mother-arms. Oh, it was beautiful! It was not a slip and a struggle and a fall into the yawning bottomless dark, but a sweet, quiet, peaceful passing out of weakness and pain into fulness of life; out of shadows into unutterable glory and light; out of our presence into the open vision of her Lord where I could not for the present follow, but the blessing of which I seemed, and still seem, in some undefinable and divinely consoling sense to share.

Thus could he sing in and of the night of his loneliness and loss. It is the writing of a man into whose deep eyes had come the shadows of a great sadness, but away in the depths of whose heart there was ringing the soft, sweet note of a joybell. For back of this cloud, the darkest yet to shadow his life, he had seen the outline of God's face, the tracing of His will.

Messages of sympathy and assurances of prayer poured in upon him from all parts of the globe. Reading these, his voice choked when he was heard to say: "Oh, this communion, this fellowship, this brotherhood and sisterhood of saints! How do sinners live? They do not live! They are dead while they live!"

A few days later, anxious as always to share with his comrades the spiritual "spoil" he had wrested from the enemy down in his own poignant valley of the shadow, he took up his pen. What he wrote was for the columns of *The War Cry,* but it was to have a wider circulation, being reprinted in a little booklet under the title, "The Consolation Wherewith He Was Comforted," and distributed widely as a cameo classic written in a victorious vein while its author was still surrounded with echoes of the words "Dust to dust, ashes to ashes."

Of this experience, his pen recorded the following:

God so helped me at the last that, when I looked into that deep grave where we buried her, it seemed more like a resurrection than a burial. There was no sting. The grave had no victory. It was only receiving the broken alabaster box of her worn little body, while her sweet spirit—like Mary's precious ointment—was with Jesus, and the perfume of her blessed life was all about us. There was a babbling brook of happiness in my heart the day we were married, but there was an ocean-current of bottomless joy and fathomless peace in my soul as we buried her. God had set Himself to comfort me. . . . I seemed, and still seem, upborne on a sea of blessedness that floods and pulses through all my soul, and in which the surges of my grief and my tears are constantly lost.

Did this attitude of soul seem callous, artificial, not consistent with human nature? Were there those who would look askance at "joy" and "blessedness" at such a time? As though anticipating this, he wrote:

What is the secret of all this blessedness, this triumph over the worst that death can do? Some will say, "It is unnatural"; but I am now writing to my comrades—Salvationists and Christian friends—who, I trust, will say, "It is supernatural." It is above nature; it is divine. It is heaven begun below. It is the work of the "other Comforter" who Jesus promised should come, and who has come forth from the Father and the Son. It is the hand of the Father stretched forth through the veil to wipe away tears and bind up broken hearts. The secret is salvation, salvation—the salvation of our God through repentance, renunciation of sin, and faith in a crucified and risen Savior, and the blessing of a clean heart, filled with His Spirit, received and kept by obedient faith.

And again we see deeply into the soul of his Christian philosophy on this subject in the following expressions made to the General under date of July 20, 1915, three and a half months after Mrs. Brengle's death:

If God's people could look upon their greatest loss as possibly their one and only supreme opportunity throughout an eternity to prove their love and loyalty and to magnify their Lord, and, instead of repining and fainting and rebelling, would look up and rejoice and count it joy for His dear sake, how it would confuse the Devil and astonish hell, rebuke unbelief, and fill the world with light!

Spiritual victory over the bitterness and hopelessness of death, however, did not give him immunity from the loneliness and hunger of life. It is the divine economy to console the present and light up the future, but memories of the past and its sweetness cannot be blotted out. While her spirit hung ever about him, fragrant, like the perfume that lingers in a room after the flowers have been taken away, her spiritual essence could never quite make up for her physical absence. Through all his days, paragraphs like the following crept into his letters:

And now I am hieing me back to my empty nest. Eleven years ago the archer came and shot down my sweet mate, and the last birdling has flown away to a nest of her own, and deep silence has fallen where there was much love and laughter and merry and affectionate bantering. There is no love in the mere four walls of a house, so I have to look up rather than out and around for love. Thank God, there is love, love fathomless, love boundless, love everlasting up there, and through obedient faith in the Lord Jesus, it comes down into my heart, and I have peace, sweet peace.

The passing of Mrs. Brengle meant that he had lost the only one in the world with whom he could hold soul converse. Many would be close in his affections, and with them he could have fellowship and communion. But she was the one, the only one, who had won him from the natural reticence of lonely farm boyhood into the complete communion of affinity. With Mrs. Brengle gone, he had no living person to whom he might go for that utter frankness of expression so noticeable in his correspondence with her.

Then, too, her death meant something else. It meant the passing, for him, of home. Though, as we have noted elsewhere, he had never known the feeling of home in the sense that most men know it, the farm at Amenia, the quarters in Portland and Worcester and a few others, had been places where he might return and find her, and, because of her, a sense of having some place to go to when worn out, body-broken, in need of rest and repose as a result of ill-health and over-labor. Here, in each of these places, was the house where she had waited for him on his return trips, the domestic spot where he could find wifely love, the bliss of childish voices. Here the cozy spot where body and soul might become relaxed; his shelter; his harbor.

But now he was harborless. Hotel loneliness—the

dreariest loneliness known to man—was thenceforth to be his. He would be entertained and billeted in many homes of his comrades, but he would never again be able to settle back into one completely and entirely his own. Not even in the homes of his children, in each of which a room was fitted cozily and comfortably for him, and where a loving welcome always awaited him, could he stifle this cry of his heart:

> *"O for the touch of a vanished hand,*
> *And the sound of a voice that is still."*

CHAPTER XXVI

THE WRITER

IF ANY would take the full measure of Brengle, he must stretch his tape along a trinity of dimensions. For in him abode these three: the preacher, the man, and the writer. To say that perhaps the greatest of these is the writer does not in any way attenuate the estimate that may have been made of him either as preacher or as man. Looked at from any angle, Brengle impressed his contemporaries as one who would live long after his demise.

His platform utterances, sublimely simple and simply sublime, were sufficient to carry him to succeeding generations. Yet, though he preached no sermon, his saintly life will win him immortality in the hearts of multitudes. Yet again, because the printed word goes farther and lasts longer than immediate personal influence, Brengle the writer will have power with men long after Brengle the preacher and Brengle the man have become only gracious tradition.

Knowing the preacher and the man, one readily recognizes the writer. He was so far from being in the slightest degree artificial that it would have been a physical impossibility for him to be one thing on the platform, another behind the scenes, and yet another between the covers of a book. In pulpit, in private, in print, he was—Brengle.

So it was that an officer in Korea, writing in *The Officer*

a prize-winning article on "My Favorite Army Book,"
could say of the author of "Ancient Prophets":

The book breathes the personality of the author; for though it has
never been my privilege to see or hear the Commissioner, by reading
his books and articles I feel that if I were to hear his voice in the
flesh it would sound like that of an old, familiar friend.

Brengle was not a creative writer in the strictly literary
sense of the term. His articles and books are largely auto-
biographical. Every word and every sentence is either
reflective of his own life—and thus a transcript of his own
heart—or of the needs of others, to deal with which he
drew upon his own experience. This made what he wrote
authentic and authoritative to an exceptional degree.

His writings, therefore, are seen to contain much of personal testimony. Writing to General Bramwell Booth in
1925, the freshly completed manuscript of "Resurrection
Life and Power" before him, he said:

I have put in much of my own experience. I look upon God's
dealings with my soul, not as something to be hidden in my own heart
for my personal comfort and guidance, but as a trust for the tempted
and hungry-hearted who will hear and read me.

Virtually all he wrote bears this stamp. In his writings
he is a doctor, skilled and experienced. With his ear to his
own heart, his hand on the pulse of human experience, and
his arm about the drooping shoulders of sinning humanity,
he wrote his prescriptions.

And, by reason of the fact that what he wrote is so much
a vital part of himself on paper, the birth of an article or
book was achieved only through travail of spirit. He himself has drawn aside the curtain to let us see him at work:

My soul has often been deeply moved while writing. Again and
again, as I have been composing an article, I have burst into tears

as I have tried to display the love and mercy of my Lord and make it applicable to the deep needs of my readers.

On more than one occasion friends came upon him at his desk, his pen in one hand gliding over the paper, his other hand supporting his head, while tears flooded his eyes and glistened on his cheeks, sobs shaking his body in tiny, spasmodic jerks.

Depth of emotion, however, does not mean that he wrote in flames of inspiration. While it is true that much which he produced bears the certain mark of having been divinely imparted, it is equally true that the propelling power of his genius more closely resembled desperation than inspiration. He said:

I seldom have a thrill while writing. It is usually a throe. I get into an agony sometimes in trying to write a little bit of an article. I can't dash things off instantly. I sweat and labor over my subject, muse upon it, feel for just the right word, study to get just the right beginning. But, when I have put down a sentence, I seldom ever change it or throw it away.

That being true, it can be said of him that he was an excellent illustration of the axiom, "Hard writing makes easy reading." His simplicity and clarity of style are the delight of the literate and the illiterate alike. There is no trace of flourish, no use of figures of speech that are merely ornate, no attempt at clever phrasing. He was simply a man of God writing because he had something he felt it necessary to say. And he said it as naturally, as clearly, as directly, as though he were conversing. Because his works are natural, clear, and direct, therefore, they are of the very soul of real literature. When occasion once arose for the discussion of the question as to who were The

Army's literary stylists, it was almost unanimously agreed that "in Brengle we have the purest stylist of them all."

* * *

In 1914, while thumbing the pages of a *War Cry*, Brengle's eye lighted upon a half-page advertisement of his books. Picking up a pair of scissors he clipped this out, pasted it in his scrap-book, and inscribed on the margin: "O Lord, scatter these little books abroad—for the feeding of Thy lambs and sheep."

"Scatter them abroad. . . ." Have they been scattered abroad? Let us see:

In number, his books—like his sermons—are not many. They are only eight—not a prodigious achievement when compared with the bulk turned out by more prolific wielders of the pen. It is not, however, the number of his works, but their big circulation that staggers the mind in its endeavor to appraise their worth and influence.

Exactly what has been their total circulation, it is impossible to say. Due to the incompleteness of The Army's record system concerning its earlier published works, and due also to the fact that these books were translated and printed in many different publishing departments over the world, it is difficult to arrive at more than an approximation. A safe and conservative estimate, however, would be a million copies. A million copies! And this takes no notice of the hundreds of thousands of paper editions, booklets made from choice portions, and reprints of certain chapters and extracts by Army and other papers and magazines the world round.

"*. . . for the feeding of Thy lambs and sheep.*" Here, then, we catch a glimpse of the imagined audience Brengle saw when he put his pen to paper. The "little people"

again! Because, in the beginning, he was called to be their
servant, he became a Salvationist. Because he carried
them on his heart when he prepared his addresses, it was
primarily to their needs and perplexities he ever addressed
himself. And, therefore, when he was writing, we are not
surprised to find here, too, it is the "little people" he has
particularly in mind. Thus it was that when he found that
his writings were being widely read by the great as well as
by the lowly, no one was so surprised as he. He said:

> The books I have written were for the people. While I was writing,
> the preachers and the high officers who might read me never entered
> my mind. The temptation with the lawyer, the doctor, or minister is
> always to think: "What will the brethren think of this?" My love
> for these little folks was such that I never thought what the ones
> higher up would think or say, if anything. And yet, in trying to
> help "little people," I found that my writings helped the "big
> people" as well. I don't know when I was more surprised than one
> day when I saw Bramwell Booth's statement in the preface to one
> of my books that these articles, of which the book was made, had
> been a great blessing to him. I had no thought that I was writing
> for Bramwell Booth; I was writing for all of God's little people!

There were others, too, for whom he did not write but
whom he blessed nevertheless. Dr. Daniel Steele, after
reading "Helps to Holiness," wrote to him saying: "I have
read your book, and I am delighted to find it has the red
cord of testimony to the cleansing Blood and Fire of the
Holy Ghost running all through. It's bound to be very
useful."

A Salvationist, on one occasion being entertained in the
home of a prominent bishop of the Methodist Episcopal
Church, noticed in the bishop's library a complete set of
Brengle's works. He made bold to comment on the fact.
"Oh, yes," said the bishop, "I buy everything that Dr.
Brengle, your great and holy apostle, writes. His books are
like refreshing showers to my soul!"

Dr. J. Stuart Holden, the celebrated English preacher, who for years was the vicar of St. Paul's, Portman Square, London, was another who came under the Brengle influence. Dr. Holden bears testimony as follows:

During my undergraduate days, Brengle's "Helps to Holiness" was put into my hands, and made a profound impression upon me. I had recently entered into an experience of the Holy Spirit's indwelling, and Colonel Brengle's teaching both enabled me to understand what God had done for me, and confirmed my confidence in His fidelity. In turn this influenced my ministry; and I have myself always endeavored to teach the More Abundant Life in the same terms. During those earlier years of my Christian service, I distributed "Helps to Holiness" to large numbers of ministers and workers. And invariably blessing followed to them also. Only once did I have the privilege of meeting the Colonel. And, brief as was my meeting with him, I carried from it the sense of having joined hands with a very true man of God, and of having received through him a benediction. Since that day he has occupied in my heart one of its highest places.

Other prominent dispensers of the Brengle evangel in book form were Paget Wilkes, the noted missionary to Japan, and his fellow-missionary, Barclay Buxton, who distributed hundreds of copies of "Helps to Holiness" throughout Japan. Wilkes, in a circular letter to friends and supporters of the missionary cause in Japan, wrote:

I would refer again to that wonderful little book of Brengle's— "Helps to Holiness." I have given it away by the hundreds. I have many verbal testimonies to the wonderful blessing it has been. One missionary writes: "I praise God for the spiritual uplift that the reading of Brengle's little book brought me." To those seeking the higher spiritual life and to those who have already found it, the book is alike a great light. If any of you have never read the little book, please get it, read it at once, and then in gratitude for the blessing which I know you will get, send me out twenty-five, fifty or one hundred copies for distribution.

The Oriental Missionary Society, too, was especially ardent in widely scattering Brengle's books. The late Anglican Archbishop of Melbourne, Australia, Dr. Harrington Lees, a great holiness teacher, recommended and personally sold and distributed many copies. The American evangelist, Joseph Owen, having taken a stock of his books with him when conducting a nation-wide series of meetings with preachers, wrote to the publishers saying: "I cannot keep enough of Brengle's books on hand to meet the demand."

In his preface to the Dutch edition of "When the Holy Ghost is Come," Dr. J. H. Gunning, eminent theologian and editor of the most widely circulated Christian weekly magazine in the Netherlands, says:

It has been my privilege, before writing this preface, to read this book from the anointed Salvationist. . . . I know the author through having read other literature of his, and I know but few warriors who make one so silent before God's face. With this capable and profound theologian, there was never any show of learning, never invectives against those who hold other opinions; so different from the armored warriors of our native country. This is so, however, not because of any ambiguous or "hovering" stand-point! For I assure you that this man holds tenaciously to the Holy Scriptures as God's infallible Word, and also to the indispensableness of the cleansing Blood of Calvary to the lost sinner. But he has an unlimited faith in the conquering power of the Truth, and does not believe that this needs the tin swords and pikes from the theologians' arsenal. With true majestic simplicity he explains the works and aims of the Holy Ghost. . . .

He reminds me very much of John Henry Newman, so far as his fineness of spirit and his original Bible commentary are concerned, but he is infinitely more cheerful than this ascetic priest. But, like Newman, he has walked with God, and the eternal world is to him the highest reality.

Many religious book stores besides those of The Army have carried, and still carry, his books in stock. An edition of 19,000 copies of "Helps to Holiness" was printed for the Keswick people in London. Organizations emphasizing the teaching of holiness have been glad to recommend them to their members. The Christian Witness Company ordered them, for many years, in lots of 800 for their evangelists and for sale at camp-meetings. The publishing house of the Nazarene Church and that of *God's Revivalist* magazine also have distributed a great many.

Occasionally, when Brengle would be "talking shop" with other ministers and authors with whom it was his habit to "swap books," would express surprise that, in conformity with an Army regulation, he had received not a cent of financial remuneration for anything he ever wrote. And the wonder would grow on them when a moment of hasty figuring revealed the tidy fortune in royalties which might have been his had he received the usual percentage which other publishing houses pay their authors. One writer, however, whose royalties from his own books provide him with a neat addition to his regular income, evidently saw the point behind the Army regulation; for he said: "To us the non-profit-sharing system of The Army might appear rather tough on Brengle, but that fact in itself forever lifts his writing above the criticism of being prompted by anything save the purest desire to bless and save."

Chapter XXVII

ASPECTS OF LATER YEARS

BRENGLE'S day may be said to have spanned the close of one and the beginning of another distinct era in the world's history.

When he began to preach, the so-called Victorian age, with its romanticism and religious emotionalism, was entering upon the last lap of its run. Side by side with the later development of those characteristic features of the era, there had sprung up a new growth of intellectual life, embracing a spirit of curiosity, of skepticism, a questing for truth based on hard, provable facts. This spirit soon led to startling discoveries in the field of science, evolving a new outlook for speculative thought and creating an insatiable hunger for fact in place of fancy. Thus was ushered in the new age of materialism, which may be said to have reached its peak state in the years immediately before, during, and after the World War.

That the spirit of an age affects the vitality of the religious life of that age, goes without saying. Test tubes, cold machinery, hard cement highways—things to satisfy man's curiosity, his demand for quick production, his desire for speed—have a way of throwing their reflections into men's souls, making them cynical, hard of countenance and heart, nervous and restless for speed and more speed. There is a vast difference between the bulk of result in soul-saving efforts during a "revival period"—when the spirit of the age quickens men's hearts with poetry and emotion—and those attending a like effort in a day when cold reason is exalted, and sentiment, religious or otherwise, is held in check.

As the new era of materialism came in, none marked its advent more quickly than did Brengle. He saw that the old day of religion softly suffused by emotionalism was past. Church attendance fell off: an affectation of personal religion was no longer held vital to one's place in society or business. The new day was practical, "hard-boiled," coldly analytical. Saintliness, to be convincing, must be the handmaiden of sanity and transparent sincerity. Brengle saw it as a day when men looked at things—science, ethics, standards, everything—cool-headedly; and religion, if it would not be outmoded, must be able to stand the same detached scrutiny.

Questions were sent his way. Would he find a change of gospel necessary to the new day? His doctrines were good for the romantic and religious era, but how now when men's ideas had undergone a hardening process?

The fact that the passing years brought no change to his doctrine is itself the measure of the timelessness of this man's message. In some matters, such as those concerned with dogmatism on the non-essentials, he had softened somewhat, as we have seen; grown more tolerant, more widely sympathetic than he was in the days of his youth. But in principle the theology of all his years was his theology of 1886.

He maintained that some things are changeless—the character of God, of sin, of the Devil; God's redemptive plan from blackest sin to whitest purity. And on these he brooked no argument, gave no quarter, admitted no change.

Because he looked upon the faith to which he had given his soul as modern, up-to-date, contemporary, it naturally followed that there was nothing about his presentation of the Gospel that caused men to think of it as anything but up-to-date. It would shine, shout, smack of freshness, newness, virility, life. Whatever of dogma he held in his later years was robust dogma which, because it concerned the essentials, was neither variable nor subject to modification.

In 1928 an officer wrote to the editor of *The Staff Review,* asking in forum whether there was "a new message for our new age." The letter was referred by the editor to Brengle and other Army leaders. Brengle replied:

Did either Luther, Fox, Wesley, or the Founder . . . ask what special message he should bring to his age? I hardly think so. Each one of these men first got a *definite burning experience of redeeming love and grace,* that filled his own heart with peace, with flaming love to God, restful confidence in Jesus, tender compassion for his fellowmen, and then, after diligent searching of the Scripture, and after much prayer, he spake as he was moved by the Holy Ghost. . . . That message of the Spirit to his own soul became his message to his age and to the ages. . . . I do not think there is any other message for any age. The emphasis upon one phase of the message or another, and the application of the message to the kaleidoscopic manifestations of sin, may vary from time to time, but the message itself is given us from heaven and is for ever one and the same. . . . Sin, too, is for ever one and the same, whatever new mask it may wear, and its wages, whatever its form, is death. . . .

The message is not to the age, but to individual men and women. . . . It is the man even more than the message that wins men. . . . Our problem, it seems to me, is not so much to find a message for the age, as to find and keep the beaming joy, the glow, the glory, the radiance and the burning love which are found alone in looking long and daily into the face of Jesus revealing the glory of God, and in humbly, joyously embracing the Cross, and following Him.

This is not the reply of an old man whom senility had slowed down while the years had gone on beyond him. Rather is it the word of a wise and seasoned veteran, who, having fought long on many battlefields, had found the enemy the same, the issues unchanged, the regulation ammunition still effective when properly used.

He knew the day to be changed, the ground to be more stony, the seed slower in springing into life. But instead of blaming the seed, he knew the fault to lie in the soil, which both sin and the season had helped to harden. So he sowed confidently on, content in the ability of his message to reproduce itself in due time in proper abundance. And God, whom he knew as the Master of all seasons, did not leave him without fruit.

His health during his latter years was, for the most part, good. With the exception of the automobile accident in 1924 and the operation in 1928, to which we have already referred, no serious ills befell him. Even into old age, he maintained the suppleness of physique and energy of motion which his bodily care and exercise had given him. In 1931, when he was nearing seventy-one, an observer watched him go through his morning exercise, and marvelled that

his vigor was that of a young man, the grace of his motions that of a skilled dancer. As he went up and down on his toes, and bent backward and forward from the waist, there was no sound of creaking joints or evidence of rheumatic muscles. He is a miracle of physical preservation, when one considers his age and the physical distress he has been through.

In these latter days, if those who looked after his physical well-being sought to slow him down, he would merely laugh at them. The late General Bramwell Booth, having written him after his operation in 1928 to "go slowly; do nothing but write, and that only sparingly," received this reply:

General, I need moral support to turn down an invitation to do meetings. If I ever say "No," it is with a sort of guilty feeling, as though I were a slacker and a lazy loafer.

His presence at camp-meetings and officers' councils was still increasingly in demand. If his comrades considered it too much to ask him to take an active part, they simply asked: "Just come and let the people look at you," feeling that the very sight of him gave spiritual tone to any gathering.

As age crept remorselessly on, whitening his beard and thinning his hair (the only places where his age was apparent), his personality took on an even softer benignity than ever. An expert on facial characteristics, studying him in 1932, found in the lines of his face and the contours of his head signs indicating

great reverence; a respect for authority; an intellectual depth with broad understanding; courage that is more of the negative nature, that gives an ability to say NO firmly; a keen sense of humor; a total lack of the crafty or secretive; but no bumps of combativeness; somewhat lacking, also, in signs of those assertive qualities usually seen in the faces of great executives or originators of new movements.

His diary covering the November period of his life is studded with prayers. An entry made in 1927 includes the following:

O Lord, as I grow old, help me to understand Thy mind for me and Thy will. I realize that each state of life—youth, manhood, old age—has its own problems. Help me to understand the mysteries of old age. I have not passed this way before. Help me to be wise, to make no mistakes, to be serene, patient, hopeful and unafraid.

On another date there is this:

O Lord, as old age overtakes me, save me from two evils: on the one hand, the querulous, critical, fault-finding habits into which so many old people fall; and, on the other, the soft, gullible spirit. Keep my eyes wide open to the weakness, foolishness, guilefulness and sin of men; yet keep my heart tender and sympathetic and hopeful. Help me to be firm and steadfast in my loyalty to truth, and always clear as to what truth is. Don't let me be deceived. Don't let me go astray the very least in my old age. Don't permit me to fall into even a little folly that, like a fly in a pot of ointment, will spoil the influence of a life devoted to Thee. Help me, O Lord.

These prayers indicate that he was very much alive to the possibility that, though he had preached to others, and had come far along the path of Grace, he might yet become a castaway. See in this further prayer how carefully he guarded against the little sins so common to old age:

Keep me, O Lord, from waxing mentally and spiritually dull and stupid. Help me to keep the physical, mental, and spiritual fibre of the athlete, of the man who denies himself daily and takes up his cross and follows Thee. Give me good success in my work, but hide pride from me. Save me from the self-complacency that so frequently accompanies success and prosperity. Save me from the spirit of sloth, of self-indulgence, as physical infirmities and decay creep upon me.

Thus praying daily and hourly, the prophet kept his passion hot and his eye single, even as he came down the decline.

But is this not the same spirit that kept him all along life's journey, rendering his calling ever more sure, his confidence in God's will for him ever more firm, his trust ever more settled? Certain it is that nothing less—no mistaken vision, no splendid enthusiasm, no transient fancy—could have enabled him to tread the decades so tirelessly, undoubtingly, pushing on through days dark and days bright, through health and unhealth, maintaining always the erect soul, the buoyant step of the conqueror. His inner compulsion, be it stated, had its roots deeper than mere sentiment or emotion. The spirit that delivered him so finally to old age had its basis in *a call*—definite, unequivocal, undiminishing.

This—only this, and nothing more, let us emphasize— can account for his arrival at the end of the road, inspired with the same passion with which he started, aglow with the same fire that inflamed his youth.

Chapter XXVIII

RETIREMENT

On June 1, 1931, a bookkeeper in an office at National Headquarters, New York, opened a record book labelled "Retired Officers, U. S. A.", found an index tab marked "B," picked up his pen and wrote the name:

Samuel Logan Brengle, Commissioner.

The date found Brengle in his room at his daughter's home in Amenia, N. Y. Here he was preparing some messages to be given to the young people at a series of summer camps where his itinerary, unimpressed by retirement decrees, was to take him.

On a bookshelf in the room where he sat writing, were a set of books. If he took down one of them, "Ancient Prophets," and turned to page 33, he could read a chapter headed "Retired." In this treatise, three years before, he had recorded his reactions to his approach to "the abyss of retirement." Then, he had written:

But is it an abyss? Will it swallow me up, and shall I be lost in its dark and silent depths? Is it not rather a sun-kissed, peaceful slope on the sunset side of life where my often overtasked body can have a measure of repose, and my spirit, freed in part from the driving claims of the War, can have a foretaste of the Sabbath calm of eternity?

Having said this, however, he had straightway seen that, though retirement might free him from the driving claims of the War, it could not free him from the driving spirit

239

of Brengle. He knew then that retirement for him would be an anomaly. He could not picture himself settling back comfortably in life's gloaming, calmly awaiting the approach of eventide. Continuing, "I do not expect to fold my hands and sit in listless idleness or vain repining when I am retired," he had forthwith laid out a program for himself. Among other things, he would

pray more for my comrades who are on the field and in the thick of the fight, . . . meditate more, . . . and read and ponder my Bible more, and try to match its wondrous truths with [my] life, . . . and by its light try to interpret the life that surges all around me. . . . Then there are letters I can write to struggling officers on the field, . . . letters to missionary officers in far-off heathen lands, letters to those who are bereaved, . . . to those . . . in pain and weariness and . . . loneliness.

As he had pondered the matter, the thought of retirement gave him less and less concern, for he saw quite clearly the breadth of the fields of labor out of which no mere (R) after his name could fence him:

I shall find plenty to do. If I can't command a corps or a division, or take part in councils, or lead on great soul-saving campaigns, I can talk to my grocer and doctor and letter-carrier about Jesus crucified and glorified, and the life that is everlasting. I can wear my uniform and go to my corps and testify, and still can take an interest in the children and young people, and maybe out of the books of my experience find some helpful life-lessons for them. In doing this, I shall hope to keep my own spirit young and plastic and sympathetic.

And, as usual, he had looked for company among his comrades in Sacred Writ. Paul in prison, John on Patmos, "even poor blind old Samson" who, "sent into dark and bitter retirement through his sin, at last groped his way back to God and wrought havoc among the enemies of the Lord and accomplished more in his death than in his life"—if these in their retirement could write ageless letters, see

and hear more wonderful and heavenly things than ever
man saw and heard before, and do more damage to the
Devil in their old age than during all the rest of their life
put together, why might not he also be productive in retirement?

These were some of the sentiments he could read in his
own book on this, the day of his own official retirement.
He must assuredly have been musing thus, for on this day
he took up his pen and appended to the chapter an anno-
tation to bring it up to date:

It was several years ago that I wrote the above. Swiftly these
years have passed, and the day of my retirement is at hand. The
snows of seventy winters are on my head, but the sunshine of seventy
summers is in my heart. The fading and falling leaves of seventy
autumns solemnize and sadden my soul, but the resurrection life up-
springing in flower and tree, the returning song birds, the laughing
brooks, the swelling rivers, and the soft, sweet winds of seventy
springtimes, gladden my spirit.

As I bend over my Bible, read and meditate, and then lift my
heart to God in thanksgiving, in praise and in prayer, I realize the
truth of Paul's words: "Though our outward man perish, the inward
man is renewed day by day."

To the officer who had been appointed to succeed him as
National Spiritual Special, Brengle, after the manner of
an Elijah casting his mantle on Elisha, wrote:

You are passing through the doors into immeasurable opportunities
of saintly and soldierly service. It is not an easy job to be National
Spiritual Special, but it is glorious beyond measure. It has kept me
busy for more than a third of a century: my head, my heart, my
hands, have been full. I have visited great corps and had crowds to
speak to, and I have visited insignificant corps and found a mere
handful of soldiers, and with but a few friends, spending days trying
to help them. Singing, preaching, praying, shouting, weeping, often
in pain and utter weariness, sometimes in deep loneliness, and with
an aching heart, but always with victory in my soul, and in the end
victory in my fightings, I have had for my reward the smile of my
Lord and the deep gratitude of saved sinners and sanctified souls.

In a hundred directions you will have opportunities that angels will covet, and joys that angels can never know—the joy of bringing sinners to Jesus and feeding the flock that He has purchased with His own blood, and the joy of strengthening the hands and comforting and inspiring the hearts of your fellow-officers. May the Lord bless you more and more, and fill your heart with sweetest peace and the comforts of the Holy Ghost. And the wisdom that is from Above will help you beyond all your past experiences to win souls!

The retirement meetings took place at the Centennial Memorial Temple, New York City, and consumed all of one day and two-thirds of another—a gigantic testimonial to the place he held in the hearts of men and women of all stations of life.

The first day, Sunday, was devoted to three public meetings—holiness, praise, and salvation—at each of which Brengle gave the chief address. General (then Commander) Evangeline Booth presided at the Sunday evening meeting, in the course of which she delivered what one reporter described as "a magnificent eulogy of a magnificent saint of God." And, in addition to the presence of highly-placed church and Army leaders, all the phases of Salvation Army pageantry were brought into play to make the occasion one befitting the prominence of the man whom all were delighting to honor. When the current *War Cry* went to press, it gave in bold headlines and minute description a record of the colorful day:

From 9 A. M. to 11 P. M. on the Sunday of Commissioner S. L. Brengle's retirement from active service, the neighborhood of the Centennial Memorial Temple was startled with Salvation activities extraordinary.

Four bands stirred the neighborhood at an early hour. Two long parades and a mammoth open-air featured the day. Great crowds attended all three inside meetings in the Temple. Between gatherings, the loud speaker of the Metropolitan Auto Battery thundered testimony and announcement, and clarioned Salvation music.

The pipe organ thundered, songs ascended from many throats, the Commander-in-Chief was on the platform surrounded by leading Commissioners and staff. . . . It was a gathering of great moment and a thousand inspirations, memorable and epochal. . . . The Commander-in-Chief accorded Commissioner Brengle the highest tribute which could be paid to any Salvationist. . . . The Commissioner himself gave the address. He was acclaimed by a standing house. . . . The day concluded at a late hour, amid scenes of great rejoicing and enthusiasm. It was a day that can never be forgotten by those who participated in its many-sided activities.

On the Monday, at noon, Brengle was the guest of honor at a luncheon with leading staff officers. And in the afternoon he was the chief speaker at an officers' council for six hundred officers and cadets.

It is notable that, of the thousands who attended the meetings of these two days, practically every one was a man, woman, or child whom Brengle had at some period particularly blessed. In many respects, therefore, the gatherings were family get-togethers of his spiritual children. Here were some who owed to his guidance their present position on the pathway of Grace. Here, too, were those whose collars bore insignia which would not have been there had Brengle not lived. And here also were many hundreds whose faltering souls had been spurred on again and again by him to higher endeavor.

Natural it was then, that, when the invitation was given, fifty-two should voluntarily move out to the altar. And just as natural was it that no sooner had the prayer-meeting begun than Brengle should be missing from the platform—where he was the honored individual upon whom this whole demonstration turned—and be found down at the penitent-form, dealing with the sinful, mingling his prayers with those of the prodigal, encouraging the weak, weeping and shouting with the victorious.

After the retirement meetings were over, Brengle himself was seen to smile genially and, squaring his shoulders and clicking his heels together in imitation of a soldier snapping into action for a fresh campaign, put the query: "Do I look retired?" In a letter written three days after his retirement function, he said with just a touch of drollery:

Well, it took them two days to get me retired. And now I am beginning all over again. In fact, I began yesterday, preaching my first sermon at the National Convention of the Christian Alliance. Calls have been coming in from the Orient and the Occident, and I already have tentative engagements which will keep me busy up to the fall of 1933. It looks like my retirement was something of a joke, doesn't it?

And, indeed, his retirement did seem to many to be "something of a joke." Barring the days when he was increasingly indisposed by "this tired old heart of mine," he was as active as ever during the ensuing two years or so. Indeed, if anything, he did more than ever. For now he felt free to go and come as he liked, to make his own engagements, to accept or reject them as he was able. And there were very few that he rejected. Calls came for his services from every quarter. Church conventions, denominational summer assemblies, colleges, and camp meetings —all seemed to feel now that, retired from his active connection with The Army, they could claim their own. He was especially powerful at the "World Conference for the Promotion of Holiness," held in Chicago in 1933.

An honor which he prized highly was his induction into the Order of the Founder. This was conferred upon him by General Evangeline Booth in New York City on September 23, 1935.

But as the days passed, he found that his body was far more tired than was his spirit. His heart refused to respond to the demands he made upon it, and he was urged by his doctors to cease entirely all public activity. It became necessary for him to take more and more frequently a heart stimulant which he called his "dynamite pills."

He found himself unable to stand the winters in the north, and took to spending them in St. Petersburg, Fla., and dividing his time in the north between the homes of his son and daughter. Here he tried to follow the doctors' orders, resting much, and busying himself between times with his enormous correspondence. To this phase of his work—always a big and important part of his service—he turned with renewed zeal. If the doctors would not allow him to do public work, he could at least sow his seed via his letters!

All through his career he had kept up a huge personal correspondence. He had a genius for letter-writing that frequently struck wonder in many less busy men when they observed the bulk of his mail. Letters requesting counsel such as the stamps could carry found their way to him from all parts of the globe. All of these he answered personally, giving to each the same careful attention one gives to the most important of documents.

In their letters to him, as at the penitent-form, people freely opened their hearts, giving him their confidences, their soul secrets. Others came not for help or advice, but just to pour out their joy over personal victories, over success in their work, over souls that had been saved through their efforts, knowing that he would be delighted with the news.

So now, with the aid of a stenographer when he could get it or writing by longhand when he couldn't, he devoted himself to his letters.

In the last year or so of his life, however, his eyes began to fail him. And of all the fleshly thorns that had pierced him in his lifetime, perhaps this was the sharpest. To be shut away from reading, severed from first-hand contact with his beloved Bible and the books he loved, to be forced to depend upon others to translate his correspondence for him—all this was painful indeed.

His affliction, however, gave him additional interest in the plight of the blind. Feeling a new kinship with them, he investigated the Braille books for the blind, and was instrumental in having several of his own works made up in the Braille method and put in libraries and other places at the disposal of those deprived of their sight.

With his descent into the "abyss of physical darkness," it became noticeable that he began to look with a degree of longing toward the Land of Light. In his correspondence of this period there was a recurring suggestion that he felt his work on earth to be nearly complete. And with this feeling, he seemed to be moved to work even more feverishly at his correspondence, signing the typed letters in a huge scrawl, and never neglecting to append in his own hand, as was ever his wont, some text or Scriptural reference that he felt would help the one to whom he was writing. One of the last letters he wrote, received by General Higgins (R) on the day of his death contained a characteristic spirit of triumph over his infirmity, as well as a portentous note of suspicion that his stay on earth was getting briefer. The following is an extract:

"My eyes are bad, and I am getting weaker, but, hallelujah! on I go to see the King in all His beauty and the Land that is afar off— and yet not far off! Glory to God in the highest!"

Chapter XXIX

SUMMONED HOME

In a New Year's message for 1936 which Major Alfred Gilliard, Editor of the London *War Cry,* had requested for his readers, Commissioner Brengle included his personal testimony:

I do not know when I have entered upon a year with sweeter peace and comfort of the Holy Spirit, or with more quiet and assured hopes, than those with which I enter this year. What the year has in store for me I do not know, but of this I am assured, that goodness and mercy shall follow me as they have all my days. Hallelujah!

What the year held for him physically was a gradual break-up of those body forces which he had for so many years subjected to such severe tasks; his eyesight would grow dimmer, his hearing would fail him, and his heart trouble would become aggravated. But spiritually he was still climbing toward new heights. Early in the year he wrote a friend:

My old eyes get dimmer. The specialist says the light will fade altogether. So I gird myself for darkness, quote James 1: 2 to 4, shout Hallelujah and go on!

And later, unable to keep an engagement which he had tentatively made, he wrote from the gathering darkness of his physical eyesight:

. . . I have sweet fellowship at times in my own room. The saints of all the ages congregate there. Moses is present, and gives

247

his testimony, and declares that the eternal God is his refuge and underneath are the everlasting arms.

Joshua arises, and declares, "as for me and my house, we will serve the Lord." Samuel and David, my dear friends Isaiah, Jeremiah, and Daniel, Paul and John and James, and deeply humbled and beloved Peter, each testify to the abounding grace of God. Luther and Wesley and the Founder and Finney, and Spurgeon and Moody, and unnumbered multitudes all testify.

Blind old Fanny Crosby cries out: "Blessed assurance, Jesus is mine!" So, you see, I am not alone. Indeed, I can gather these saints together for a jubilant prayer and praise meeting almost any hour of the day or night. Hallelujah forever, and glory to God!

Thus jubilantly could he come down the long decline that would lead in a little while to the quick Up-turn of his ascending.

The end came as he would have wished it—serenely, with his house in order, and in the bosom of his beloved children and their families. He had just returned from Florida two days before. While seated at the supper table in the home of his son, George, at Scarsdale, N. Y., on the evening of May 18th, an unusually severe heart attack seized him.

Taken to his room, he retained consciousness for three and a half hours, while a doctor was summoned and absent members of the family called. All seemed to sense that this was the last of his long seige with a constantly weakening heart. He did not respond to the treatment given by the doctor, and near midnight he sank into a coma.

But before he lost consciousness, even while the doctor was working over him, he beamed upon them out of eyes that had lost three-quarters of their sight and quoted his "texts." These little verses that had been his struts and stays in all his lifetime supported him now as he prepared to stem the current of Death's river. The particular text that was on his lips as he entered into the unconscious condition from which he never emerged on earth was: *"The angel of the Lord encampeth round about them that fear him . . ."*

For thirty-eight hours he was in the coma before his spirit left the body. News of his condition was flashed around the world, and Salvationists of all nations went to their knees in petition that he be spared. But he did not rally. During those long hours he lay still, seeming scarcely to be breathing, his prophet-like countenance as benign almost as in death. Only once did watchers by his bedside see a look of animation steal over his features. It was on the day before his passing, May 19th, his wedding anniversary. And for just a brief moment there seemed to pass across his face the shadow of a smile. . . .

The next day, at 1:30 P. M., his spirit took its flight.

Word that he was gone, flashed around the world, was met with startled incredulity on the part of the thousands upon thousands who loved him. It just did not seem possible that this man, upon whom so many depended for spiritual light and instruction, was theirs no more to call upon. Telegrams, cables, and messages by every other means of transmission poured in upon the family.

The funeral service, conducted three days later by General E. J. Higgins (*R*) in the Centennial Memorial Temple, New York City, drew a huge crowd of comrades and friends desirous of paying him tribute.

In death, he was surrounded by comrade officers with whom he had engaged in many a conflict against sin. Beside General and Mrs. Higgins, there were Commissioners McIntyre, Damon, Parker and Holz, as well as other high-ranking officers of all four of America's Territories. In the audience too were many hundreds whom he had blessed and helped during his long lifetime.

General Booth herself was only kept from being present

by a campaign upon which she was engaged in Switzerland. But she sent a beautiful and characteristic message. It began: "It is fitting that one who has made Spring to break in countless multitudes of souls should be laid to rest amid the flowers of May . . ."

The funeral itself bore no trace of gloom; those present sorrowed not as those without hope. The opening words of General Higgins' masterful funeral address sounded the pitch for the occasion when he said: "I want to strike a note of gratitude, a psalm of praise, for the life of this great man." The General spoke of the departed prophet as "the dearest comrade a Salvationist ever had, as a friend, as a counselor, as a great soul-lover and soul-winner, as a writer, as a Salvationist, as a saint."

Other speakers on the program were Commissioners McIntyre and Parker. The former, dramatically leaning over the casket and addressing himself to the deceased, said: "We're going to cherish your memory, Brengle, and we here and now dedicate ourselves to living up to your high teaching!"

Following Commissioner McIntyre's eulogy, Commissioner Damon read telegrams and messages from persons all over the world, small and great, high and low, telegrams that reflected a cross-section of all the varied types and classes of human beings to whom his high ministry ever appealed.

The interment was at The Army's beautiful plot at Kensico, N. Y., and was conducted by Colonel Walter F. Jenkins (R).

But just prior to the funeral a very touching ceremony was held in the home of George Swift Brengle at Scarsdale. "Before father went on his trips," said Mr. Brengle, "he always had family prayers with us." So before the casket left the house on its last journey, the Brengle family knelt around the remains of their illustrious forbear. His favorite portions of Scripture were repeated, and verses of his best-loved hymns were read.

Many lovely tributes were paid to the Commissioner, all of which would make most interesting reading if there were room in this volume to quote them. But perhaps the most touching was that written in a letter from his son, George, who said:

"I can't find it in my heart to grieve for father. I grieve for myself, and for those he loved, for we shall not see him again for a while. But for him death was the best and happiest of a long, long number of home-comings. It was something that in a very real sense he had lived for, particularly in the years since Little Mother died. May 19th was their wedding anniversary, and I think of them now as on a second honeymoon, in 'the Land that is fairer than day.'"

POSTLUDE

". . . and your old men shall dream dreams."

IT HAS been recorded that on the very borderland of the Beyond, watchers at his bedside saw his face take on a look of benignity and peace; that once even there seemed to flit across his face the shadow of a smile . . .

Why does he smile? Of what is he thinking?

In this room, during the long hours of his coma, there have been visitors. And they have talked, in whispers, of the towering totality of his work. Catching sight of a row of his books, they perhaps mention that these printed evangels of his have fallen from the presses more than a million strong, have winged their way over the civilized world in many languages, have winnowed their way into the hearts of millions.

And waiting here by his bedside as life lingers, commenting upon this career that began in frontier obscurity and is ending upon a platform as wide as the world and as broad as the hearts of men, it is likely that they speculate upon the countless thousands who have bowed at his penitent-form, upon the innumerable multitudes who count him their spiritual parent.

And perhaps, in the secret chambers of his consciousness, he hears them. And perhaps their whispered words start his dreams, beckoning him to come for a walk down the yesteryears. Such dreams can start with recent events and trail back, far back into dim and misty memories that are preserved now for him only as vanishing pictures and faintly echoing voices.

Beginning at his retirement, with its many eulogies from small and great, he can go back step by step—back through the years of his constant labors at home and abroad, with their thousands of platforms and their thousands of penitent-forms—back to the trying days of the American "split," and his appointment as Spiritual Special —to Boston and the tough's brick—to Danbury and the "big Negro and little hunchback"—back to the Training depot and the boots that needed blacking—to the Founder's office and the skeptical words: "You belong to the dangerous classes"; back to the library of the Swift home, with its apple-blossoms, its scent of lilies-of-the-valley, and Lily standing beside him repeating the marriage covenant—to the room in Boston Theological Seminary, and his personal Pentecost—to the bleak Illinois prairie and its happy circuit-rider; back to Providence and the room in the Narragansett Hotel where he answered the call to preach—to DePauw and the companionable walks and eager talks of law ambitions with Beveridge—to long and drab days on the farm; back, clear back, indeed, to a night spent in a clearing beside a wilderness trail in southern Indiana, to the campfire blazing and his mother reading from the Bible a passage concerning God's promise to Abram, and to the sleepless hours beneath the open sky with the Bible words twisting and turning in his mind. . . .

Here, perhaps, his dream halts to dwell a while in this place of his early vision. "The stars . . . so shall thy seed be" was language that a boy in the grey dawn of his life's early morning could not understand. But as his evening has drawn on, the stars have come out. They are many; too many, indeed, for any man to number; so many that only God can number them.

Now, therefore, the words no longer twist and turn in his mind. Now he understands. And in the evening light, the multiplied promise of his morning, he bows his heart and is glad. . . .